AN AUTOPSY
OF THE UNITED STATES

An Analysis of What Killed the Original
American Ideals
and the Possibility of a Resurrection

G. Michael Cocoris

AN AUTOPSY OF THE UNITED STATES

An Analysis of What Killed the Original
American Ideals
and the Possibility of a Resurrection

G. Michael Cocoris

© 2024 by G. Michael Cocoris
All rights reserved. This publication may not be reproduced *for sale* (in whole or in part, edited, or revised) in any way, form, or means including, but not limited to, electronic, mechanical, photocopying, recording or any kind of storage and retrieval system, except for brief quotations in printed reviews, without the written permission of G. Michael Cocoris, 2016 Euclid #20, Santa Monica, CA 90405, michaelcocoris@gmail.com, or his appointed representatives. Permission is hereby granted, however, for the reproduction of the whole or parts of the whole without changing the content in any way for *free distribution,* provided all copies contain this copyright notice in its entirety. Permission is also granted to charge for the cost of copying.

Unless otherwise indicated, all Scripture quotations are taken from the New King James Version ®, Copyright © 1979, 1980, 1982 by Thomas Nelson, Inc. Used by permission. All rights reserved.

TABLE OF CONTENTS

PREFACE   1

Chapter 1

THE BIRTH OF THE UNITED STATES   5

The Revolutionary War	6
The Political Thinking	12
The Religious Environment	25
Clarification	33

Chapter 2

LIFE IN THE ORIGINAL U.S. SOCIETY   37

The Bible was Respected	37
God was Acknowledged	48
People Believed in Moral Responsibility	58
The Traditional Family was the Norm	62
Christianity influenced Education	64
Capitalism was the Economic System	70
The Rule of Law was the Rule	75
The Sanctity of Life was Accepted	79

Chapter 3

DEATH IN THE U.S. SOCIETY   91

Discrediting the Bible	91
Dethroning God	97
Discounting Moral Responsibility	102

Decline of the Traditional Family	106
Dumbing-down Education	112
Drifting away from Capitalism	125
Deserting the Rule of Law	136
Destroying Life	139

Chapter 4

LIFE AFTER DEATH IN THE U.S. SOCIETY   147

Respect the Bible	149
Rely on the Lord	154
Recognize Moral Responsibility	157
Reestablish the Traditional Family as the Norm	158
Rethink Education	160
Regulate Some Economic issues	161
Reinforce the Rule of Law	164
Reclaim the Sanctity of Life	165

Chapter 5

CONCLUSION: HOPE FOR THE U.S.   169

The Divided State of America	169
Hope for the Divided State	170

BIBLIOGRAPHY   175

Preface

Anyone who has lived as long as I have is aware that the United States has changed in the last 60 years. When I was young, I heard older people say the same thing. They thought the U.S. had changed in the past 60 years, and the generation before them said the same thing. That makes me wonder what the U.S. was like at the beginning and how it has changed from then until now. For me, what caused the change is equally interesting.

Spiritual Ideals The answers to these questions are in the history of the *ideals* in U.S. society. The Pilgrims, who came on the Mayflower, and the Puritans, who came shortly after the Pilgrims, had *spiritual* ideals. Their ideals were based on the Bible. For them, the Bible is the Word of God. The God of the Bible is the Creator of heaven and earth and the Bible contains the moral standards by which people should live. The colonialists who came later were not theologically monolithic. They had their differences. They were Episcopalians, Congregationalists, Presbyterians, Quakers, Baptists, and Roman Catholics, but they respected the Bible, acknowledged God as Creator, and believed that all should live a virtuous life.

Political Ideals The Founding Fathers of the U.S. had *political* ideals. They united the thirteen colonies, led the Revolutionary War, and drafted the Declaration of Independence, the Constitution, and the Bill of Rights. The committee members of Thomas Jefferson, John Adams, and Benjamin Franklin drafted the Declaration of Independence. George Washington was commander-in-chief of the Continental Army. John Jay, John Adams, and Benjamin Franklin negotiated the Treaty of Paris (1783) that ended the Revolutionary War. George Washington was president of the Constitutional Convention (May 24 to September 17, 1787). The Constitution of the United States relied heavily upon the Constitution of New York (1777) and the Constitution of Massachusetts (1780). John Jay and others drafted the Constitution of New York and John Adams was the principal author of the Constitution of Massachusetts. James Madison, Alexander Hamilton, and John Jay authored the *Federalist Papers*, advocating the ratification of the Constitution.

Thus, the Founding Fathers included at least Benjamin Franklin, Thomas Jefferson, James Madison, Alexander Hamilton, John Jay, George Washington, and John Adams. Others could be added. The Founding Fathers did not agree with each other on all the political details, but as will be shown, they respected the Bible and believed there is a God who gives people inalienable rights. They also believed that all citizens should live virtuous lives.

Secular Ideas Beginning in the latter part of the 19th century, a number of *secular* ideas were introduced. Thinkers such as Julius Wellhausen, Charles Darwin, Sigmund Freud, Soren Kierkegaard, John Dewey, Karl Marx, John Maynard Keyes, Milton Friedman, etc. developed ideas that slowly changed the thinking and attitudes of *people in general* (hereafter called "society") in the U.S. Thus, these thinkers became the opinion shapers of *society*. As a result, the opinions and attitudes prevalent in society today in the U.S. radically differ from what they were at its founding.

Woodrow Wilson said, "A nation which does not remember what it was yesterday does not know what it is today, nor what it is trying to do. We are trying to do a futile thing if we do not know where we came from or what we have been about" (Wilson, cited by Federer, p. 697).

My primary purpose is to inform. When I asked a few friends to read the first draft, some were surprised at what the Founding Fathers said. Most were unaware of the impact of thinkers such as

Preface

Wellhausen, Kierkegaard, and Dewey. Some appreciated the simple explanations of the economic theories of Adam Smith, Karl Marx, John Maynard Keynes, and Milton Friedman.

Beyond providing information, my purpose is to provoke thought. As a nation, we need to think about where we are and where we are headed in light of what made the U.S. great in the first place.

G. Michael Cocoris
Santa Monica, CA

Chapter 1

THE BIRTH OF THE UNITED STATES

The land now known as the continental United States was occupied initially by American Indian tribes. European immigration began in the 16th and 17th centuries. Virginia was established as a colony in 1607. The Pilgrims landed at Plymouth and created the Plymouth colony in 1620. New Amsterdam, later renamed New York, was founded in 1624. The Puritans originated the Massachusetts Bay colony in 1629, which became the state of Massachusetts in 1788. Lord Baltimore established Maryland in 1632, and Roger Williams established Rhode Island in 1636. These colonies were followed by Connecticut (1636; officially established in 1662), New Hampshire (1638; officially chartered in 1679), Delaware (1638; established by the English in 1664), North Carolina (1663), South Carolina (1663), and New Jersey (conquered by the English in 1664). William Penn founded Pennsylvania in 1681, and James Oglethorpe founded Georgia in 1733.

Most people in the colonies were British citizens who settled along the Atlantic Coast east of the Appalachian Mountains. During this period, the colonies ran themselves with Britain sending token governors. From 1690 onward, the British government began exercising more and more control over the colonies through new taxes and governors. Eventually, a conflict arose between the colonies and Britain, which culminated in the Revolutionary War and the formation of the U.S.

What *events* led up to the war? What were the political *ideals* that shaped the government of the U.S.? Why did the people support the political ideals of the Founding Fathers?

The Revolutionary War

The French and Indian War (1754-1763) In 1754, a war began between the French with their colonies and Indian allies and the British with their colonialists and Indian allies. It ended in 1763 with the Treaty of Paris. This war is significant because the British colonists organized their own army, Britain ended up with enormous territorial gains in North America, and Britain doubled their debt.

The Stamp Act (1765) To raise money to pay off their debt in 1765, the British Parliament passed the first direct tax on the colonies. The Stamp Act required that many printed materials in the colonies be produced on stamped paper produced in London, which had an embossed revenue stamp. Printed materials included legal documents, magazines, newspapers, playing cards, and many other types of paper used throughout the colonies. Because of the reaction of the colonialists, the Declaratory Act (1766) repealed the Stamp Act. Still, it declared the right of Parliament to govern the colonies in all cases whatsoever (Allison, Lecture 16, p. 108).

The Townshend Acts (1767-1768) In 1767, Charles Townshend proposed a series of acts passed by Parliament, such as The New York Restraining Act, The Coercive Act, The Revenue Act, etc. The New York Restraining Act forbade the New York Assembly and the governor from passing any new bills until they agreed to comply with the Quartering Act of 1765, which required New Yorkers to provide housing, food, and supplies for British troops.

The Indemnity Act concerned tea. The British Parliament had given the East India Company a monopoly on importing tea from China, and the East India Company paid a 25% tax on all the tea they imported (1698). Parliament had also passed a law that required the colonies to import tea only from England (1721). However, citizens in England and America were able to buy smuggled Dutch tea at much lower prices. In response, Parliament passed the Indemnity Act to help the East India Company compete against smuggled Dutch tea. It lowered the tax on tea consumed in England and gave the East India Company a 25% refund on the tea exported to the colonies. The Indemnity Act also provided general warrants that could be used to search private property for smuggled goods. The Revenue Act taxed glass, lead, painters' colors, paper, and tea to help offset the loss of revenue from The Indemnity Act.

The colonists were outraged by the Townshend Acts. They argued that the new taxes violated the British Constitution, which said that British subjects could not be taxed without the consent of their elected representatives, and the colonies did not have elective representatives in the British Parliament. This was "taxation without representation." Furthermore, the right to be secure in one's property was a right in Britain. The colonists responded with protests and boycotts. Merchants organized a non-importation agreement.

The Boston Massacre (March 5, 1770) Beginning in 1768, British troops were stationed in Massachusetts to support British officials and enforce unpopular British legislation. In early 1770, more than 2,000 British soldiers occupied Boston, a city of 16,000. In protest of British taxes, Bostonians often vandalized stores selling British goods. Skirmishes between the colonists and the British soldiers were increasingly common. Fights broke out between the two. On the snowy evening of March 5, 1770, a lone British soldier guarded the King's money in the Custom House on King Street. A crowd gathered, hurling insults at him and threatening violence. Reinforcements arrived. When one soldier fired, other shots followed. Three members of the crowd were killed instantly and eight were wounded, two of whom later died of their wounds. This "Boston Massacre" further incensed the colonists.

The Boston Tea Party (December 16, 1773) In 1773, approximately 86% of the tea sold in America was smuggled Dutch tea. In London, the East India Company was struggling financially and had warehouses full of tea. On May 10, 1773, Parliament passed the Tea Act to reduce the amount of tea held by the East India Company and to undercut the price of illegal tea. The Act granted the East India Company the right to *ship its tea directly* to America without going through British wholesalers. The colonists recognized the implications of the Act's provisions, such as taxation without representation, so a coalition of merchants, smugglers, and artisans mobilized opposition to the delivery of British tea in America. The East India Company's authorized dealers were harassed and many efforts to prevent the tea from landing were successful. In Boston, this resistance culminated in the Boston Tea Party on December 16, 1773, when a band of Bostonians dressed as Mohawk Indians boarded tea ships anchored in the harbor and dumped their tea cargo overboard, worth millions of dollars today.

The Coercive Acts (March 28, 1774) In response to the Boston Tea Party, Parliament passed the Coercive Acts, also known as The Intolerable Acts, designed to punish Massachusetts for its resistance. The Coercive Acts were a series of four acts, including The Boston Port Act, which closed the port of Boston until damages from the Boston Tea Party were paid, The Massachusetts Government Act, which restricted Massachusetts' democratic town meetings and turned the governor's council into an appointed body, The Administration of Justice Act, which made British officials immune to criminal prosecution in Massachusetts, and The Quartering Act, which required colonists to house and quarter British troops on demand, including in their private homes as a last resort.

The Coercive Acts took self-government away from Massachusetts. The British appointed General Thomas Gage as governor of Massachusetts. Parliament hoped the Coercive Acts would cut Boston and New England off from the rest of the colonies and prevent unified resistance to British rule. Instead, other colonies rushed to the city's defense by sending supplies and forming their own Congress to discuss British misrule and mobilize resistance to it. Hence, the First Continental Congress was held.

The First Continental Congress (September 5, 1774) After Parliament passed the punitive Coercive Acts in response to the Boston Tea Party and the British Navy instituted a blockade of Boston Harbor, delegates from 12 of the 13 British colonies met in Philadelphia from September 5 to October 26, 1774, for the First Continental Congress. The delegates included George Washington, John Adams, Samuel Adams, Patrick Henry, and John Jay. The delegates discussed how the colonies should collectively respond to coercive British actions. A plan to create a Union of Britain and the Colonies was rejected. They did not demand independence from Britain.

The delegates denounced taxation without representation and the maintenance of the British army without their consent. They issued a declaration of the rights due to every citizen, including life, liberty, property, assembly, and trial by jury. They agreed to impose an economic boycott on British trade and drew up a petition to the King pleading for a redress of their grievances and repeal of the Coercive Acts. They also voted to meet again in May 1775 to consider further action. In the meantime, the appeal to the king had no effect and violence erupted.

The Battle of Lexington (April 19, 1775) About 700 British Army regulars in Boston were given secret orders to capture and destroy colonial military supplies stored by the Massachusetts militia at Concord. The colonists had received word weeks before that their supplies might be at risk and had moved most of them to other locations. On the night of April 18, 1775, hundreds of British troops marched from Boston toward Concord, Massachusetts to seize the arms reserve. Warning of the troop movements was sent from Boston to the militia. The Army's initial mode of arrival was signaled from the Old North Church in Boston using lanterns to communicate "one if by land; two if by sea." Paul Revere and other riders sounded the alarm.

The colonial militiamen began mobilizing to intercept the British Redcoats. On April 19, 1775, the first shots were fired at Lexington, Massachusetts. Eight militiamen and one British soldier were killed. Outnumbered, the militia retreated, and the British troops proceeded to Concord, searching for supplies. At the North Bridge in Concord, approximately 400 militiamen engaged 100 British soldiers, resulting in casualties on both sides. The outnumbered British retreated and rejoined the British forces in Concord. Years later, poet Ralph Waldo Emerson described the first shot fired by the militia at the North Bridge in his "Concord Hymn" as the "shot heard round the world."

The Second Continental Congress (May 10, 1775) After the battles of Lexington and Concord, the Second Continental Congress convened on May 10, 1775. This time, Benjamin Franklin and Thomas Jefferson were among the delegates. The delegates voted to form a Continental Army and unanimously appointed George Washington as commander-in-chief. On July 2, 1776, the Continental

Congress adopted the Lee Resolution, which declared independence from Britain. The Declaration of Independence was signed two days later. This Congress functioned as the provisional government through March 1, 1781. It managed the war effort, drafted the Articles of Confederation and the U.S. Constitution, and secured support from foreign nations. France entered the war in 1778 and Spain joined the war the following year. In early 1782, Parliament voted to end all offensive operations in America and on September 3, 1783, Britain and the United States signed the Treaty of Paris, in which Britain agreed to formally end the war and recognize the sovereignty of the United States.

The treaty of 1783 gave the new nation the land to the Mississippi River, except for Canada and Florida. The Articles of Confederation had established a central government but had not provided for an executive officer or for collecting taxes at the national level, which required the consent of the states. So, in 1787, a convention in Philadelphia wrote the Constitution and adopted it. It was ratified in 1788 and took effect in 1789. The Bill of Rights was added in 1791. The Purchase of the Louisiana Territory from France (1803) doubled the size of the United States.

Conclusion The colonies endured oppressive British rule for ten years before the Revolutionary War. Among other things (see the 27 grievances in the Declaration of Independence), the colonists were being denied their rights of self-government, being taxed without representation, being forced to house British troops, even in their own homes, etc. They attempted to resolve these issues peacefully, but the British started the armed conflict when they killed five men at the Boston Massacre on March 5, 1770. Eight more were killed at Lexington on April 19, 1775. "Separation from Great Britain was not selected as the American course of action until two years **after** King

George III had drawn the sword and sent armed troops against his own citizens in America" (Barton, p. 93, bold type his).

John Witherspoon (1723-1794), a signer of the Declaration of Independence, said, "On the part of America, there was not the most distinct thought of subverting the government or hurting the interest of the people of Great Britain, but of defending their own privileges from unjust encroachment; there was not the least desire of withdrawing their allegiance from the common sovereign [King George III] till it became necessary and indeed was his own choice" (Witherspoon, *The Works of John Witherspoon,*, vol. IX, p. 250, cited by Barton, pp. 93-94).

John Quincy Adams (1767-1848), the sixth President, said, "There was no anarchy.... The people of the North American Union and its constituent States were associated bodies of civilized men and Christians in the state of nature, but not anarchy. They were bound by the laws of God, which they all, and by the laws of the Gospel, which they nearly all acknowledge as the rules of conduct" (Adams, in an address delivered on July 4, 1821, cited by Barton, p. 94).

The Political Thinking

Where did the political leaders, the Founding Fathers, get their ideals for the establishment of the U.S. government? During the First Continental Convention in June 1787, Benjamin Franklin said, "We have gone back to ancient history for models of government, and examined the different forms of those republics.... And we have viewed modern states all around Europe" (from *The Papers of James Madison*, cited by Barton, p. 219). Historians agree the Enlightenment, also known as "The Age of Reason," influenced the Founding Fathers. It was a philosophical movement that dominated the world of ideas during the 18th century. Based on the sovereignty of reason, the Enlightenment advanced such ideals as liberty and constitutional government.

To be more specific, a group of political scientists pinpointed the particular thinkers who influenced the Founding Fathers by analyzing more than 15,000 political writings from the Founding Era (1760-1805). The goal was to identify the sources cited during the debate in establishing the American government. From the 15,000 writings, the researchers isolated 3154 quotations and documented the original sources of those quotations (see Donald S. Lutz, *The Origin of American Constitutionalism*. Baton Rouge: Louisiana State University Press, 1988, cited by Barton, p. 219). The Bible was cited four times more than any other source and 20 times more often than English philosopher John Locke. It accounted for 34% of the direct quotations in the political writings of the Founding Era (Barton, p. 231).

In the foreword of *The New England Pulpit and the American Revolution*, Joel McDurmon says the vast quantity of quotations from the Bible in the study appeared in publications during the earlier part of that era, years before the Philadelphia convention. The authors of the study themselves said that the closer to the Convention, "the Bible's prominence disappeared" (McDurmon, p. ix; see also his "The Framers and Their Alleged Frequent Bible Quotations"). The Bible may not have been as prominent among the Founding Fathers as it had been a few years earlier, but, as will be shown, they spoke about it and respected it.

Montesquieu The most frequently invoked political source was the French philosopher Montesquieu. His *The Spirit of Laws* (1748) had a powerful influence on the thinking of the founders (Barton, p. 220). Charles-Louis de Secondat, Baron de La Brčde et de Montesquieu (1689-1755), generally referred to as Montesquieu, was a French judge, author, and political philosopher. He was born into a Roman Catholic family and attended a Catholic college, but he married a Protestant and later became a Freemason. In *The Spirit of Laws,* after describing three types of governments, Montesquieu discusses various subjects pertaining to each of the types. (A translation of this two-volume work is posted at https://oll.libertyfund.org/titles/montesquieu-complete-works-vol-1-the-spirit-of-laws/simple#lf0171-01_label_745. To view vol. 2, change "vol-1" to "vol-2.) Here are quotations from *The Spirit of Laws* with the topics in bold print.

Montesquieu begins *The Spirit of Laws* by acknowledging that there is a **God.** Also, in the first chapter of the first book, Montesquieu discusses the **nature of man.** He says, "An intelligent being [man], incessantly transgresses the laws established by God" and "Such a being might every instant forget his Creator; God has, therefore, reminded him of his duty by the laws of **religion**." In other words, Montesquieu bases his theories on God's existence, man's sinfulness, and the necessity of religion. He speaks of the "wickedness of man" in Bk. VI, Ch. XVII (see below).

Montesquieu says, "There are three **species of government**, republican, monarchical, and despotic.... A republican government is that in which the body or only a part of the people is possessed of the supreme power; a monarchy is that in which a single person governs by fixed and established laws, and a despotic government is that in which a single person directs everything by his own will and caprice" (Bk. II, Ch. I).

Favoring **the republican form** of government over the others, Montesquieu asserts that "the **supreme power" resides in the people** and it is "a fundamental maxim, in this government, that the people should choose their ministers; that is, their magistrates," adding, "They can tell when a person has fought many battles, and been crowned with success; they are therefore very capable of electing a general" and "They can have better information in a public forum than a monarch in his palace" (Bk. II, Ch. II). The people, however, must have **virtue**. Montesquieu said, "When virtue is banished, ambition invades the minds of those who are disposed to receive it, and avarice possesses the whole community" (Bk. III, Ch. III). Therefore, **education** is required and what must be taught is virtue, which is defined as *"the love of the laws and of our country"* (Bk. IV, Ch. V, italics his).

To **protect themselves against external force**, several smaller states should "agree to become members of a larger one, which they intend to establish" (Bk. IX, Ch. I). "The Canaanites were destroyed by reason they were petty monarchies, that had no union nor confederacy for their common defense" (Bk. IX, Ch. II). "Political **liberty** does not consist in unlimited freedom. In governments, that is, in **societies directed by laws**, liberty can consist only in the power of doing what we ought to will, and in not being constrained to do what we ought not to will" (Bk. XI, Ch. III). In Bk. XI, Ch. VI, Montesquieu taught the **separation of powers** with the government structure. (In Federalist 51, Madison argued for the separation of powers and checks and balances.)

"The **Christian religion**, which ordains that men should love each other, would, without doubt, have every nation blest with the best civil, the best political laws; because these, next to this religion, are the greatest good that men can give and receive" (Bk. XXIV, Ch. I). "From the characters of the Christian and Mahometan [Islam] religions, we ought, without any further examination, to embrace the one, and reject the other.... The Mahometan religion, which speaks only by the sword, acts still upon men with that destructive spirit with which it was founded" (Bk. XXIV, Ch. IV). "The Catholic Religion is most agreeable to a Monarchy, and the **Protestant** to a Republic" (Bk. XXIV, Ch. V).

Montesquieu's ideas include the following: 1) There is a Creator. 2) Humans are incessant transgressors. 3) Humans need religion as a restraint and Christianity is the best religion (Islam is to be rejected and Protestantism is the best form of Christianity for the republican form of government). 4) Republicanism is the best form of government. 5) For republicanism to work, the people must be virtuous. 6) For republicanism to work, there must be a separation of powers into legislative, executive, and judiciary (there will be no life and liberty without the separation of powers). 7) To protect themselves from external forces, small states should band together into a larger state.

John Quincy Adams noted, "At the time of the Declaration of Independence, Montesquieu was one of the most recent and esteemed writers upon government and he had shown the division of powers to be essentially necessary to the preservation of liberty" (Adams, an Oration delivered on July 4, 1831, cited by Barton, p. 221). Montesquieu was not alone in the belief that the powers of government should be kept separate. Guelzo points out that England's government was a three-way system of checks and balances: king–lords–and commoners (Guelzo, p. 21). Locke insisted that the best form of government was the three-part government that protected property through the rule of law (Guelzo, lecture 6).

Barton added the "separation theory is rooted in the biblical concept in Jeremiah 17:9 that people naturally tend toward corruption. Following the religious teachings of the day, it was generally accepted that the unrestrained heart of man moves toward moral and civil degeneration (what the Puritans, Calvinists, and others called the 'depravity of man'). Thus, it was logical that society would be much safer if all power did not repose in the same authority. If the power is divided and one branch becomes wicked, the others might still remain righteous and, thus, be able to check the wayward influence" (Barton, p. 221).

Blackstone Sir William Blackstone (1723-1780) was the second most invoked political authority during the Founding Era. He was an English judge, law professor, and author of the four-volume *Commentaries on the Laws of England* (1765-1769), which were the law books for the U.S. Senate (*Debates and Proceedings in the Congress of the United States*, p. 65, cited by Barton, p. 222). Blackstone is cited as a legal authority in the writings of John Adams, Thomas Jefferson, John Marshall, James Madison, Joseph Story, et al. (Barton, px. 222, fn.).

Justice James Iredell, who was appointed to the Supreme Court by George Washington, said Blackstone's views were relied upon by those who formed the Bill of Rights (Iredell, in his charge to a grand jury in 1799, cited by Barton, p. 223). In 1799, Iredell said that for nearly 30 years, Blackstone's commentaries had been "the manual for almost every student of law in the United States" (Barton, p. 223). In 1810, Thomas Jefferson said that the U.S. lawyers used Blackstone with the same dedication and reverence that the Muslims used the Koran (Jefferson, *The Writings of Thomas Jefferson* vol. XII, p. 392, cited by Barton, p. 223).

The two phrases **"the laws of Nature"** and "the laws of **Nature's God**," which appear in the introduction to the Declaration of Independence, are in Blackstone's works. Blackstone said the laws of man's Creator are called the laws of nature and are "binding over all the globe, in all countries, at all times" and "the doctrines thus delivered we call the revealed or divine law and they are to be found only in the Holy **Scriptures**.... Upon these two foundations, the law of nature and the law of revelation, depend all human laws, that is to say, no human laws should be suffered to contradict these" (*Commentaries,* vol. 1, pp. 39, 41-42, cited by Barton, p. 223). The idea of "laws of nature" is a biblical concept. Paul said, "When Gentiles, who do not have the law, by nature do the things in the law, these, although not having the law, are law to themselves, who show the work of the law written in their hearts" (Romans 2:14-15).

Locke John Locke (1632-1704), a British philosopher, was the third most cited author in early American thought. He is considered one of the most influential Enlightenment thinkers. His two most famous works are *An Essay Concerning Human Understanding* (1689) and *Two Treatises of Government* (1690, but probably composed before 1683). The Founders used many of his writings, especially his *Two Treatises of Government.* Locke influenced Alexander Hamilton, James Madison, Thomas Jefferson, and other Founding Fathers.

Locke taught that all men have **God-given rights**, including life, liberty, and property, that these rights cannot be taken away, that people form governments by entering into a **social contract**, that rulers have authority by consent of the governed, that the duty of government was to protect the rights of the people, and that for the government to work, people must follow the laws that government makes. If the government should fail to protect those rights, its citizens have the **right to overthrow** that government. In 1689, Locke argued, "The **church** itself is a thing absolutely separate and distinct from the Commonwealth" (Stevens, pp. 10-11).

Historian Allen C. Guelzo's explanation of Locke is that using reason, rather than tradition, as a guide for political life, Locke was concerned with throwing off the yoke of the monarchy. He begins imagining people in a "state of nature" before a government exists. All are born equal and the issue was survival. Therefore, they used their labor to provide food, clothing, and shelter, which became their "property." At that point, the danger is that their property might be taken away from them. Therefore, people invent "government," a security patrol and supervisory board, for the sole purpose of security. Since people invent government, if that government does not operate according to some law, they have the right to establish a new government. Locke warned that the government people create will degenerate and decay, set aside the rule of law, and grab for more and more power, thus reducing liberty for the people (Guelzo, Lecture 6; see p. 21).

Locke's theory of **social compact** appears in the Declaration of Independence, where it says that governments "derive their just powers from the consent of the governed." (Barton, p. 224). Locke also said, "The **law of nature** stands as an eternal rule to all men, legislators as well as others. The rules that they make for other men's actions must ... be conformable to the Law of Nature, i.e., to the will of God" and "Laws humans must be made according to the general laws of Nature and without contradiction of any positive law of **Scripture,** otherwise they are ill-made" (Locke, *Two Treatises*, Bk. II, p. 285, cited by Barton, p. 224).

Barton points out, "So heavily did Locke draw upon the **Bible** in developing his political theories that in his first treatise on government he invoked the Bible one thousand three hundred and forty-nine times [1349]; in his second treatise, he cited it one hundred fifty-seven times [157]" (Barton, p. 225). Many have pointed out that the political concept of a **compact** is compatible to the biblical concept of the covenant.

Hooker Richard Hooker (1554-1600) was a British theologian and legal philosopher from whom Locke specifically drew his ideas. Like Locke, Montesquieu, and Blackstone after him, Hooker began by establishing the **origin of the law**. He said consider "the nature of law in general ... namely, the law whereby the **Eternal Himself** doth work. Proceedings from hence to the law, first of Nature, then of **Scripture**, we shall have the easier access into these things which come after to be debated" (Hooker, *The Works of the Learned and Judicious Divine, Mr. Richard Hooker*, vol. I, p. 148, cited by Barton, p. 226). Hooker believed that Man's **natural rights** came from the **Bible**. He said, "The Scripture is fraught even with the laws of Nature" and referred to Gratian, who said, "**Natural rights** were contained in "the Books of the Law and the Gospel" (Barton, p. 226).

Gratian (died ca. 1155) is the Father of Canon Law. At the time, the Roman Catholic Church had no uniform law, even though Popes had made legal decisions and councils had issued decrees. After years of study, he wrote *Concordia discordantium canonum*(*Harmony of Conflicting Canons*, a.k.a. "Gratian Decrees"), which became the most important book on Church law. Almost 3800 chapters covering ten centuries contain statements from the church fathers, papal decisions, counsel decrees, excerpts from Roman laws, theological opinions, and many contradictions.

Gratian systematically arranged material according to the subject matter and applied emerging techniques of logic and dialectics to solve conflicting decrees. He taught a new way of interpreting and applying the law. Although it was never officially adopted by the Roman Catholic Church, it became the most important legal guide for popes, bishops, and ecclesiastical courts until it was finally replaced by a new code of Canon Law in 1917.

Hooker declared, "Let piety [civil government] acknowledge itself indebted to **religion**.... So natural is the union of religion with justice that we may boldly deem there is neither where both are not" (Hooker, *Works*, vol. I, p. 427, cited by Barton, p. 226).

Hume David Hume (1711-1776), a British philosopher and author of *Treatise of Human Nature* (1739-1740), is the fourth most cited political authority during the Founding Era. He did not approach government theory from a biblical perspective. The Founders did not rely upon his political theories; they criticized and refuted them. John Adams called him an "atheist, deist, and libertine [one not under the restraint of law or religion]" (Adams, cited by Barton, p. 227). However, Benjamin Franklin and Hume were close friends (Allison, p. 57).

Several other political philosophers were esteemed. Alexander Hamilton recommended Grotius, Puffendorf, Locke, and Montesquieu. Alexander Hamilton, John Witherspoon, Benjamin Franklin, James Wilson, Samuel Adams, and numerous other Founders respected Grotius and Puffendorf (Barton, pp. 228-229). *Grotius* Hugo Grotius (1583-1645, a Dutch lawyer, theologian, and author of *Concerning the Law of War and Peace* in 1625), wrote the first definitive text on international law and the *Truths of the Christian Religion* (1627). He argued that "What **God** has shown to be His will that is law" (Grotius, *Commentary on the Law of Prize and Booty*, vol. I, p. 8, cited by Barton, p. 229). "He also said, "It may seem impossible for any state so long to subsist unless it was upheld by a constant particular care and by the power of the Divine hand" (Grotius, *The Truths of the Christian Religion*, p. 20, cited by Barton, p. 229).

Puffendorf Barton Samuel de Puffendorf (1632-1694), professor of law and nature at universities in Sweden and Germany, contended that if civil law violated the rise that law of God, men were required by God to disobey that civil law (Puffendorf, *Of the Law of Nature and Nations*, Book I, p. 68, cited by Barton, p. 229).

These "thinkers" have been listed in the order of the number of times they were quoted. Chronologically, the list would start with Gratian (died ca. 1155) followed by Hooker (1594-1597), Grotius (1625), Puffendorf (1672), Locke (1690), Montesquieu (1748), and Blackstone (1765-1769). My political science professor friend says the concept of natural law can be found in the teachings of the ancient Greeks such as Plato, Aristotle, Cicero, etc., and in the writings of the early Christians such as Justin Martyr, Ambrose of Milan, Augustine, etc.

In modern times, Hooker spoke of natural rights and law being first founded in nature and then in Scripture (1594). In 1672, Puffendorf said no government could survive without acknowledging God and if civil law violated God's law, God required disobedience to civil law. In 1690, Locke spoke about the law of nature, unalienable rights, the social compact (the consent of the governed), and limited government. In other words, the *ideas* of natural rights, unalienable rights, natural law, divine law, a social contract, limited government, and disobeying civil law were in printed materials that influenced the Founding Fathers almost a century before 1776. Closer to their time, ideas were in print concerning the nature of man, the need for religion, specifically Protestant Christianity, and the necessity of separating powers into the legislative, executive, and judicial branches of government (Montesquieu, 1748).

To say the same thing another way, the thinkers who most influenced the Founders, Montesquieu, Blackstone, Locke, Hooker, and others, taught: 1) There is a God. 2) Humans are sinful. 3) Nature contains natural law and natural rights. 4) Nature's God revealed His will and law in the Scripture. 5) To have a just society, there must be religion. 6) Government should have a separation of power between the legislative, executive, and judicial branches. 7) There needs to be a social contract between the government and the governed; the government governs by the consent of the governed. These ideas are either in the Bible or compatible with the Bible.

Jefferson In this intellectual environment, Jefferson wrote the Declaration of Independence. The Declaration is a simple document with profound ideas. It consists of a preamble, a list of 27 grievances against British rule, and a conclusion. In the preamble, Jefferson declares 1) It is self-evident that all men are created equal and possess rights given to them by the laws of nature and nature's God that cannot be taken away from them. 2) Governments are instituted to secure these rights, including the rights of life, liberty, and the pursuit of happiness. Governments derive their just powers from the consent of the governed. 3) Whenever any government becomes destructive of these ends, it is the people's right and duty to alter or abolish it and institute a new government, which will most likely grant them safety and happiness. 4) Prudence dictates that long-established governments should not be changed for light and transient causes, and experience has shown that people are more disposed to suffer than to right the wrongs by abolishing the government to which they are accustomed. But when abuses and usurpations reduce people to absolute despotism, it is their right and duty to throw off such government and to provide a new government for their future security.

The 27 grievances detail the abuses, usurpations, and absolute despotism of British rule. Many of the colonies were required to submit their laws to the king for approval, but the king withheld his consent, effectively vetoing colonial legislation. The colonists wanted additional migration, but the king prevented new migration. The British Army was permanently stationed in the colonies and the colonial governments were required to help pay for their support. The British forbade the colonies to trade with other nations (France, Spain, etc.). Taxation was without representation.

The conclusion states: 1) The colonies had repeatedly petitioned for redress, only to be met with a tyrant who was "unfit to be the ruler of a free people." 2) The colonies frequently had appealed for justice, but the British "have been deaf to the voice of justice." 3) Therefore, "appealing to the supreme Judge of the world," the united colonies declare their right "to be free and independent states," their total separation "from all allegiance to the British crown and all political connections between them and the state of Great Britain, and their establishment of independent states "with a firm reliance on the protection of divine Providence."

As Barton pointed out, "The Declaration of Independence was actually a duel declaration: a Declaration of **Independence** from Britain and a Declaration of **Dependence** on God" (Barton, p. 106, bold type his).

Conclusion The Declaration of Independence contains political ideas from the thinkers of the day, such as people possess rights given to them by the laws of nature and nature's God that cannot be taken away from them, Governments are instituted to secure these rights, Governments derive their powers from the consent of the governed, and whenever any government violates becomes their legitimate authority, people have the duty to abolish government and institute a new government. Dependence on God is needed.

The political ideas that produce not only the Declaration of Independence but also the Constitution include: 1) God-given laws are indicated in nature ("The laws of nature and nature's God"). 2)

God-given laws contain inalienable rights (see "inalienable rights" in the Declaration). 3) Self-government is through a social contract between the people and the state ("Governments are instituted ... deriving their just powers from the consent of the governed"). 4) Government is to secure the rights of people ("To secure these rights, Governments are instituted among Men"). 5) Government governs by the consent of the governed ("deriving their just powers from the consent of the governed"). 6) Since people are sinful, the government's power needs checks and balances. 7) For republicanism to work, citizens must have virtue. 8) For people to be virtuous, there must be religion. 9) The best religion is Christianity. 10) When the government violates laws that give people their inalienable rights, they have a duty to abolish that government and establish a new one.

The bottom line is all have God-given rights that are to be protected by the government, which governs by the consent of the governed. In the words of Abraham Lincoln, the U.S. was "conceived in liberty and dedicated to the proposition that all men are created equal." Thus, the political ideals of the U.S. boil down to: all are created equal, all have the right of self-government, and all have liberty. In short, the U.S. is built on the ideals of liberty and limited government. Those *political* ideals made the U.S. great.

The Religious Environment

The Pilgrims and the Puritans The Pilgrims who came to America on the Mayflower (1620) and landed at Plymouth were Separatists; they wanted to separate from the Church of England. About half of the 120 who made the trip died the first winter. A few years later, the Puritans, who came and settled in Salem and Boston, were

Congregationalists; they were loyal to the Anglican Church but thought the church needed to be purified. They were well educated; more than 100 of the first Puritans who came to America had been educated at Oxford or Cambridge. Within six years of landing, the Puritans founded Harvard (1636). Forty to fifty thousand Puritans came so that by 1776, 75% of colonialists in New England had Puritan roots (Bill Petro, "What is the difference between Puritans and Pilgrims?" at https://www.quora.com/profile/Bill-Petro).

The Great Awakening During what is called "the First Great Awakening," thousands of people in the 13 colonies were converted to Christ. In December 1734, Jonathan Edwards preached a series of sermons on justification by faith, emphasizing the need to experience conversion. In his essay "A Faithful Narrative of Surprising Work of God in the Conversion of Many Hundred Souls in Northampton, and Neighboring Towns and Villages of the Country of Hampshire" (titles were long in those days), Edwards said, "There was scarcely a single person in the town, young or old, left unconcerned about the great things of the eternal world. Meetings were thronged." Within a year in Northampton, Massachusetts alone, a town of some 200 families, approximately 300 people were converted. By the following year, the revival had spread to the cities of South Hadley, Suffield, Sunderland, Deerfield, Hatfield, West Springfield, Long Meadow, Enfield, Westfield, Northfield, East Windsor, Coventry, Stratford, Ripon, Tolland, Hebron, Bolton, and Woodbury.

From 1738 to 1770, George Whitefield, an Englishman, made seven tours to America, preaching throughout the colonies. He preached to crowds numbering into the thousands. In his autobiography, Benjamin Franklin says he measured the crowd that Whitefield spoke to in Philadelphia and estimated that he preached to 30,000 people. Many thousands were converted. Franklin says,

"It was wonderful to see the change that soon made in the manners [behavior] of our inhabitants; from being thoughtless or indifferent about religion. It seemed as if all the world were growing religious; so that one could not walk thro' the town in an evening without hearing Psalms sung in different families of every street" (Franklin's autobiography is posted at http://nationalhumanitiescenter.org/pds/becomingamer/ideas/text2/franklinwhitefield.pdf.). It has been estimated that about 80% of all the people in the colonies heard him preach at least once (Stevens, p. 5). The response to Whitefield's gospel preaching was so great that churches could not hold all the people (Federer, p. 245).

Benjamin Franklin built an auditorium for George Whitefield to preach in when he came to Pennsylvania. After the meeting, Franklin donated the auditorium to be the first building of what became the University of Pennsylvania. A bronze statue of George Whitefield still stands in front of that building (Federer, p. 239, 245; Google a picture of it).

The Christian Population The U.S. Census Bureau estimates that, in 1776, when the Declaration of Independence was signed, the population of the 13 colonies was 2.5 million. Approximately 98% of the colonists were Protestant Christians, 1.9% were Roman Catholics, and fewer than 1% (2500 people) were Jews (Kosmin and Lachman, pp. 28–29). When the first formal U.S. census was completed in 1790, the population of the new nation was approximately 3.89 million, including almost 700,000 slaves, which was about 18 percent of the population (see https://www.census.gov/history/www/through_the_decades/fast_facts/1790_fast_facts.html).

John Quincy Adams said, "They [the people of the North American Union] were bound by the laws of God, which they all, and by the laws of the Gospel, which they nearly all, acknowledged as the rules of their conduct" (Adams, in an address delivered in 1821, cited by Barton, p. 94). In a debate in the British Parliament over the American resistance, Sir Richard Sutton read from a letter written by a Crown-appointed governor in America, which said, "If you ask an American, 'Who is his master?' He will tell you he has none, nor any governor but Jesus Christ" (from a book written by Hezekiah Niles in 1822, cited by Barton, p. 96).

Righteousness These Christians believed that moral responsibility was indispensable to civil government. Based on the Bible, they would no doubt say that righteousness is also necessary for greatness. Proverbs 14:34 states, "Righteousness exalts a nation, but sin *is* a reproach to any people." Commentator William MacDonald points out, "In order for a nation to be great, its leaders and people must have upright, moral characters known for their righteousness. Corruption, graft, bribery, 'dirty tricks,' scandal, and all forms of civil unrighteousness bring disgrace to a country." Notice he said that for a nation to be great, its people and government must be righteous. Benjamin Franklin said, "Virtue alone is sufficient to make a man great, glorious, and happy" (Federer, p. 244).

To put righteousness into focus from a biblical perspective, note the three kinds of righteousness. **Instinctive righteousness** is the instinctive human desire for what is righteous. For example, all citizens want "accountability" of government officials. From a biblical point of view, while it is true that human beings do some righteous things, all humans fall short of God's standard of righteousness; they are sinners before God. So, since sinners cannot produce the kind of righteousness that God demands, He provides what theologians call **imputed righteousness**. It is the righteousness of God imputed to people (Luke 18:9-14; Romans 3:28; 2 Corinthians 5:21; Philippians 3:3-9), that is, when people trust Jesus Christ for the gift of eternal life, God *declares* them righteous. They stand before God clothed in the righteousness of God! In the Sermon on the Mount, Jesus speaks about **internal righteousness**. The Pharisees defined righteousness as an external act. Internal righteousness depends on God's grace for the enablement to do what He commands.

To be more specific, God's kind of righteousness begins at the point of faith. Abraham "believed in the Lord, and He [the Lord] accounted it to him [Abraham] for righteousness" (Genesis 15:6). The New Testament explains that all have sinned (Romans 3:23). Jesus Christ died for such sins and rose from the dead (1 Corinthians 15:3-5). When people *trust Jesus Christ for the gift of eternal life* (John 3:16; 1 Timothy 1:16), they are not only guaranteed heaven ("eternal life"), they are declared righteous (Romans 4:5). In other words, people are righteous *before God* because the righteousness of Christ is given to them. (2 Corinthians 5:21). This is the biblical teaching of justification by faith (Romans 3:28), popularly called conversion. After trusting Christ for the gift of eternal life, believers develop practical righteousness (doing what is morally right) by being obedient to the Lord (Proverbs 14:2; Romans 6:16). The Lord has given believers His Word to instruct them on how to live a righteous life (2 Timothy 3:16) and gives them the power to do what He commands (Philippians 4:13).

When many people living righteous lives are the dominant influence in a nation, that nation is at its finest, its greatest. "Righteousness exalts a nation" (Proverbs 14:34). On the other hand, when an individual or a nation is not living by personal moral responsibility, they degenerate into lying, cheating, shoplifting, stealing, bribery, immorality, etc.

The Preaching of Politics At the time of the American Revolution, the country was not only filled with Christians who believed in personal moral responsibility but also the vast majority of those Christians had been influenced by political preaching from the pulpit. Bill Petro goes so far as to say that sermons were one of the causes of the Revolution. He says, "During the colonial era of America, ministers delivered approximately 8 million sermons, each lasting 1-1.5 hours. If you were a 70-year-old citizen, you would have heard some 7,000 sermons, totaling nearly 10,000 hours of concentrated listening. This is about ten undergraduate degrees worth of lectures. Many of these sermons in the later Colonial period were about liberation from England. Clergy molded public opinion by political sermons" (Petro; "In what ways did The Great Awakening influence the American Revolution?" https://www.quora.com/profile/Bill-Petro).

Based on her research of colonial sermons, tracts, pamphlets, and other publications, Alice M. Baldwin wrote her doctoral dissertation at the University of Chicago. In 1928, she wrote *The New England Clergy in the American Revolution*, the first part of which was based on her dissertation. Joel McDurmon edited her book and entitled it *The New England Pulpit and the American Revolution, When American Pastors Preach Politics, Resistance to Tyranny and Founded a Nation on the Bible* (2014/2019). The following material from Alice Baldwin is taken from the 2014 edition.

Long before 1763, because New England clergy preached political ideas, such as natural rights, constitutional law, social contract, government bound by the law, and the right of resistance to the government when it transcends its authority, every churchgoing New Englander was familiar with these concepts (Alice Baldwin, p. 2). From the Old Testament, New England ministers gleaned illustrations of covenant relations, the limitations placed on rulers, the natural rights of people, etc. From the New Testament, they received authority for the liberties of Christians, the relationship to those in authority over them, and the right of resistance. Ministers drew their theories from a multitude of sources from the Greek and Roman writers of their day, but "the source of greatest authority and the one most commonly used was the Bible" (Alice Baldwin, p. 16). "Indeed, there was never a principle derived from more secular reading then was not strengthened and sanctified by the Scriptures" (Alice Baldwin, p. 10). These pastors proclaimed that God planted "natural rights" deep in the heart of men (Alice Baldwin, p. 20) and that the law of nature was an unwritten law that the Bible helps to make clear and discloses to its fullest extent (Alice Baldwin, p. 21), and that God's relationship with men was determined by a covenant or compact (Alice Baldwin, p. 18, who points to the theological covenant of works with Adam and the theological covenant of grace). Also, "the Congregationalists and the Baptist, who made up perhaps four-fifths of churchgoing New England, believed that the church could only exist by a covenant, a sacred and binding agreement or compact made by the members with each other and with God" (Alice Baldwin, p. 26).

Long before 1763, the New England clergy also developed an elaborate theory of political government based on the law God revealed in natural law and the written word (Alice Baldwin, p. 29). "A government which did not have the good of the people at heart did not have the sanction of God.... This was the starting point ... for the limitations upon rulers" (Alice Baldwin, p. 31). This argument, identical to Locke's, is that governments are limited by the purpose for which they are founded, namely, the good of the people. Except for the Jews, God did not specify any type of government. Man could choose any type provided the purpose of government and was not inconsistent with the divine law (Alice Baldwin, pp. 31-32).

"Without law and obedience to law, there would be no liberty" (Alice Baldwin, p. 47). Rulers must preserve the life, liberty, and property of the people or else act in opposition to God's law. "From the middle of the seventeenth century, this [life, liberty, and property] is a common phrase, especially liberty and property.... No one can fully understand the American Revolution and the American constitutional system without a realization of the long history and religious associations that lie behind these words without a realization that for a hundred years before the Revolution, men were taught that these rights were protected by divine, inviolable law" (Alice Baldwin, p. 50). "Moses believed that the people must submit to rulers as long as they kept within their legal limits" (Alice Baldwin, p. 51). Nothing in Scripture supports unlimited submission (Alice Bowman, p. 57).

"Probably the most fundamental principle of the American constitutional system is the principle that no one is bound to obey an unconstitutional act.... This doctrine was taught in fullness and taught repeatedly before 1763.... No single idea was more fully stressed, no principle more often repeated, through the first sixty years of the eighteenth century than that the government must obey the law and that he who resists one in authority who is violating the law is not himself a rubble but a protector of the law" (Alice Baldwin, p. 212).

"All through the New England colonies, the ministers were helping to spread the theories of the philosophers and to give them religious sanction. Thus, when the trouble with England came to a head, New Englanders were accustomed to thinking and arguing for their rights in terms of natural law, the Constitution, the government by consent, and the right of resistance, and believed that they were doing so by following the injunctions of God" (Alice Baldwin, p. 213). "There is not a right asserted in the Declaration of Independence which had not been discussed by the New England clergy before

1763" (Alice Baldwin, p. 213).

When Massachusetts was in the throes of adopting the federal Constitution, General Benjamin Lincoln wrote to George Washington, 'It is very fortunate for us that the clergy are pretty generally with us. They have in this state a very great influence over the people.' So might the leaders of the Revolution have said not only in Massachusetts but in all of the New England colonists" (Alice Baldwin, p. 216).

The widespread preaching of politics during the founding era does not mean that all the denominations participated. "Congregationalists (Puritans) were the most active. Anglicans were loyalists. However, 2/3rds of those who signed the Declaration of Independence were Anglicans. Quakers were generally pacifists…. Presbyterians were the first to accept the Declaration of Independence and identify with the Revolution. Baptists were intensely loyal to England and suffered for it in Rhode Island. Methodists, whose founder John Wesley opposed the Revolution at the time, were despised as loyalists" (Petro; "In what ways did The Great Awakening influence the American Revolution?" https://www.quora.com/profile/Bill-Petro).

Conclusion When the U.S. was founded, the *population* comprised an overwhelming number of Protestant Christians. Therefore, *Christian values influenced U.S. society in the sense that the people at least respected the Bible, acknowledged there is a Creator, and believed in the morality of the Bible.*

Clarification

The Point Christian *values* influenced the original *society* of the U.S. Society is a group of people sharing the same geographical or social territory, subject to the same political authority and dominant cultural expectations. The issue is not politics; it is public opinion.

The Clarification To say that *Christian values* influenced the *society* of the U.S. is not to say the U.S. was a Christian nation, although the Supreme Court once said that it was. In 1892, in *Church of the Holy Trinity v. United States,* the Supreme Court unanimously held that "this is a Christian nation." With due respect, the U.S. has never been a Christian *nation*. A Christian nation is one whose *government* financially supports a particular Christian denomination. As Louis XIV (1638-1715), king of France, famously said, "One king, one faith, one law." England could be called a Christian nation; it financially supports the Church of England. The idea that a nation could have more than one religion, even more than one Christian denomination, was considered "lunacy until the American Revolution" (Atwood, p. 17). Some of the thirteen colonies had an established church, meaning state taxes supported the church. Those could be called "Christian" colonies, but the U.S. was never a Christian *nation;* the Constitution prohibits the U.S. from establishing a national church.

To say that *Christian values* influenced the *society* of the U.S. is not to say that it was a perfect nation. It took a Civil War to eliminate slavery and a constitutional amendment to give women the right to vote.

To say that *Christian values* influenced the *society* of the U.S. is not to say that all of the leaders or all the people were "converted" in the biblical sense of the term or practiced biblical Christianity. Some of the most well-known Founding Fathers had moral flaws. Some of them, as well as many other citizens, were slave owners. This discussion is not about the Christianity of individuals; it concerns *Christian values* influencing the *original society* of the U.S.

To say that *Christian values* influenced the *original society* of the U.S. is to say that from the beginning, the U.S. was a nation made up mostly of Protestant Christians, who influenced the nation's *society*. It is to say that most people *respected the Bible, acknowledged God, at least as Creator, and believed in biblical morality.* That degree of righteousness and its result originally made the U.S. great. "Righteousness exalts a nation" (Proverbs 14:34).

As a result of those core beliefs (Bible, God, and moral responsibility), the traditional family was the norm, students were exposed to Christianity, capitalism (the private ownership of property, etc.) was the economic system, the rule of law was the rule, and, in one sense (abortion), the sanctity of life was accepted.

Zoroastrianism is an illustration of religion influencing *society*. Zoroaster was an ancient Persian spiritual leader who founded Zoroastrianism, which taught that the only God was the Creator. Zoroastrianism challenged the existing traditions and eventually became the dominant religion in Persia. Even those who did not practice Zoroastrianism "grew up shaped by a culture that valued simple ethical ideas such as telling the truth" (Peter Davidson, "Achaemenid Empire," *Ancient History Encyclopedia*, www.ancient.eu/achaemenid_Empire/.).

John Adams wrote to Thomas Jefferson, "The general principles on which the fathers achieved independence were .... the general principles of Christianity.... Now I will avow that I then believed, and now believe, that those general principles of Christianity are as eternal and immutable as the existence and attributes of God" (Adams, *Works*, vol. X, pp. 45-46 to Thomas Jefferson dated June 28, 1813, cited by Barton, p. 134).

In 1821, John Quincy Adams declared, "The highest glory of the American Revolution was this; it connected in one indissoluble bond the principles of civil government with the principles of Christianity"

(Federer, p. 18).

Dennis Prager (1948-), a contemporary radio talk show host who is Jewish, has said, "Those Judeo-Christian values have made America the greatest experiment in human progress and liberty and the greatest force for good in history" (Prager, "The Case for Judeo-Christian Values VIII").

Summary: The *events* such as the Stamp Act, the Townsend Acts, the Boston Massacre, the overbearing rule of the British Crown, the Battle of Lexington, etc. (see the 27 grievances of the Declaration of Independence), led to the Revolutionary War, but beyond those events, political *ideals*, pastors preaching political ideals, and the influence of Christian *values* produced the American Revolution.

The U.S. *began* as a great nation because of its political and spiritual ideals. The political ideals were based on liberty and limited government. The spiritual ideals were that the Bible was respected, God, at least as Creator, was acknowledged, people believed in the kind of morality expressed in the Bible (the Ten Commandments), and, as a result, the traditional family was the norm, students were exposed to Christianity, capitalism was the economic system, the rule of law was the rule, and, in one sense, the sanctity of life was accepted. That is the kind of righteousness that made the U.S. great.

That is a bold claim. Can it be substantiated? Can it be demonstrated that Christian values influenced the original *society* in the U.S.? Do those values still influence American *society* today? If *society* today is no longer like the original *society*, what happened?

Chapter 2

LIFE IN THE ORIGINAL U.S. SOCIETY

In the beginning, U.S. society was influenced by Christian values, as opposed to other religions or secular humanism. That influence lasted well into the 19th century.

The Bible was Respected

The Bible Once upon a time, people in the U.S. respected the Bible. That is not a fairytale; it is a fact. Even Thomas Jefferson, who rejected the supernatural element in the Scripture, admired the moral standards in the Bible. In a letter dated June 17, 1804, written to Henry Fry, Jefferson said, "I consider the doctrines of Jesus as delivered by himself to contain the outlines of the sublimest system of morality that has ever been taught" (Jefferson, cited by Federer, p. 326; Millard, p. 99).

Christopher Columbus (1492) In his book entitled the *Book of Prophecies*, Christopher Columbus (1451-1506) wrote, "He [the Holy Spirit] ... consoled me through His holy and sacred Scriptures ... they inflamed me with a sense of great urgency.... No one should be afraid to take on any enterprise in the name of our Savior if it is right and if the purpose is purely for His holy service" (Columbus, cited by Barton, p. 2). Columbus also wrote that he sought new lands to "bring the Gospel of Jesus Christ to the heathens" and "the Word of God to unknown coastlands" (https://www.usaheritage.org/index.html). Clearly, Columbus respected the Bible.

Protestant Reformation (1517) A Jewish author, David Horowitz, argues that "America is the logical, if not inevitable, development of the Protestant Reformation." He says the two core doctrines of the Protestant Reformation were "justification by faith" and "the priesthood of all believers." Justification by faith is based on the idea that, since people are sinful by nature, they can only be saved by God's grace. "This led logically to the American idea that government requires a system of checks and balances to restrain the devious impulses and desires of its citizens and officials. As James Madison, one of the principal framers of the Constitution, put it: 'If men were angels, no government would be necessary'" [*Federalist* No. 51] (Horowitz, p. 42).

"The concept of 'the priesthood of all believers' led directly to the principle at the heart of the Declaration of Independence, that "all men are created equal" and endowed with rights by their Creator—rights no government has the authority to deny" (Horowitz, p. 43). The idea that all people are created equal and endowed by their Creator with unalienable rights led to the abolition of slavery and the enfranchisement of women…. Without the founders' belief in God—fiction or not – America could not exist" (Horowitz, p. 44).

Where did the Protestant Reformation get the doctrines of justification by faith and the priesthood of the believer? The Bible!

Mayflower Compact (1620) The Christian roots of the U.S. go back to the *Mayflower Compact*. Aboard the Mayflower, the pilgrims signed the famous compact, which states, "Having undertaken for the glory of God, and the advancement of the Christian faith, and the honor of our king and country, a voyage to plant the first colony in the north part of Virginia; do by these presence, solemnly and mutually, in the presence of God, and one another, covenant and combine ourselves together into a civil body politic, for our better ordering and preservation, and furtherance of the ends of aforesaid" (*Mayflower Compact,* cited by Millard, p. 19). Where did the pilgrims get the concepts of planting a colony for the glory of God and the advancement of the Christian faith? The Bible!

The Pilgrims Who were the Pilgrims? Their story starts in England. By about 600 A.D., England was a Roman Catholic nation and King Henry VIII (reigned 1509-1547) was originally a Roman Catholic. When he wanted to divorce his wife and the Roman Catholic Church would not let him, Henry declared himself the head of a new national church called the Church of England. Although he and his daughter, Queen Elizabeth I (reigned 1558-1603), changed a few things in the new church, some felt that too many of the practices of the Roman Catholic Church were retained. They wanted to purify the church to make it more biblical. These people were called "Puritans." Another group went even further. Believing that the new Church of England was beyond reform, they separated from the Church of England. Thus, they were called "Separatists." At the time, being part of any church other than the Church of England was illegal. So, when the Separatists were persecuted with harassment, fines, and even jail, they fled to Holland and, from Holland, sailed to America on the Mayflower, which arrived in Plymouth Harbor in 1620. In other words, the Puritans wanted to purify the Church of England, but the "Separatists," believing the church was beyond reform, became pilgrims who journeyed from England to Holland and from Holland to Plymouth. What motivated the pilgrims? The Bible!

Connecticut Constitution (1639) The "Fundamental Orders of Connecticut," the first written constitution in the colonies, stated, "Knowing where a people are gathered together the word of God requires that to maintain the peace and union of such a people there should be an orderly and decent Government established according to God, ... to maintain and preserve the liberty and purity of the Gospel of our Lord Jesus" (the full text of the "Fundamental Orders" is posted at http://morganhighhistoryacademy.org/GC%202%20Fundamental%20Orders%20of%20Connecticut%201639.pdf).

The Founding of Rhode Island (1636) Roger Williams (1603-1683) was a Puritan minister who was banished from the Massachusetts Bay Colony because of his radical views on religious freedom that were based on the New Testament. He founded the Providence Plantations (1636), which became Rhode Island. He paid the Narragansett Indians for the land, advocated the separation of church and state, and was one of the first abolitionists. In 1638, he founded the first Baptist church in America, which is today the First Baptist Church of Providence, Rhode Island. His belief in religious freedom and the separation between church and state inspired the founders of the U.S.

Williams wrote, "It is the will and command of God that, since the coming of his Son the Lord Jesus, a permission of the most Paganish, Jewish, Turkish, or anti-Christian consciences and worships, be granted to all men in all nations and countries; and they are only to be fought against with that sword which is only in soul matters able to conquer, to wit, the sword of God's Spirit, the word of God" (https://www.swarthmore.edu/SocSci/bdorsey1/41docs/31-wil.html). He also said, "The sovereign, original, foundation of civil power lies in the people; and it is evident that each government as are by erected and established, have no more power, nor for no longer time, then the civil power or people consenting and agreeing shall trust them with" (Alice Baldwin, p. 36).

The Founding of Pennsylvania (1681) When he was 22 years old, William Penn (1648-1718) was converted from atheism to

Christianity after hearing a sermon. He joined the French Society of Quakers and was imprisoned three times for preaching the Word. While in prison in the Tower of London, Penn dreamed of starting a colony where biblical truth could be sought, free from persecution. (Millard, p. 37). His father, Admiral Sir William Penn, gave him the tract of land now known as Pennsylvania (Penn's Wood). William and his followers landed in the New World in 1681 and, shortly after that, founded Philadelphia, the city of brotherly love. Although William Penn had been given the entire state of Pennsylvania by the Crown of England in 1682, he purchased the land from the Indians rather than taking it (Millard, pp. 37-38). William Penn's well-known "Frame of Government" stated, "that all persons ... having children ... shall cause such to be instructed in reading and writing, so that they may be able to read the Scripture and to write by that time they attain to 12 years of age" (Millard, p. 44).

The Liberty Bell (1752) In 1751, the Pennsylvania Provincial Assembly commissioned the Liberty Bell to hang in the new State House in Philadelphia. The State House was later renamed Independence Hall. The bell was cast in London and delivered in August 1752. A verse from Leviticus is engraved on the Liberty Bell: "Proclaim liberty throughout all the Land unto all the inhabitants thereof" (Leviticus 25:10). In the 1830s, abolitionist societies adopted the bell as their symbol. They dubbed it the "Liberty Bell." Where did the Liberty Bell get its slogan about proclaiming liberty? The Bible!

Delaware Constitution (1776) The Delaware Constitution required every office-holder to make and subscribe to the following declarations, "I, A. B., do profess faith in God the Father, and in Jesus Christ His Only Son, and in the Holy Ghost, one God, blessed forevermore, and I do acknowledge the Holy Scriptures of the Old and New Testament is to be given by divine inspiration"

(Millard, p. 388).

Maryland Constitution (1776) The Maryland Constitution required every officeholder to "subscribe [to] a declaration of his belief in the Christian religion" (Millard, p, 389).

North Carolina Constitution (1776) The North Carolina Constitution provided: "No person who shall deny the being of God or the truth of the Protestant religion, or the divine authority of either the Old or New Testament, or who shall hold the religious principles incompatible with the freedom and safety of the State, shall be capable of holding any office or place of trust or profit in the civil department within the State." That provision remained in force until 1835 when it was amended to change the word "Protestant" to "Christian." That amended Constitution remained in force until it was revised in 1868 and in that version, the persons disqualified from holding office were "all persons who shall deny the being of Almighty God" (Millard, p. 389).

New Hampshire Constitution (1784 and 1792) The New Hampshire Constitution required that senators and representatives be of the "Protestant religion," and that provision remained in force until 1877 (Millard, p. 389).

Continental Congress Because of a shortage of Bibles, the Continental Congress imported 20,000 Bibles (*Journal of the Continental Congress*, vol. VIII, p. 735, September 11, 1777, cited by Barton, p. 109). Later, since the shortage of Bibles remained a problem, on January 21, 1781, a publisher requested permission to print Bibles on his presses in America, pointing out that his Bibles would be "a neat addition of the Holy Scriptures for the use of schools" (from the introduction to *The Holy Bible as Printed by Robert Atkins and Approved and Recommended by the Congress of the United States Of America in 1782*, cited by Barton, p. 113).

Years later, Strickland asked, "Who will charge the government with indifference to religion when the first Congress of the States assumed all the rights and performed all the duties of a Bible Society long before such an institution had an existence in the world?" (W. P. Strickland, *History of the American Society from Its Organization to the Present Time*, 1849, pp. 20-21, cited by Barton, p. 114).

The Constitution (1788) James Madison, who was educated in Reformation theology at the College of New Jersey, later renamed Princeton University, was the architect of the U.S. Constitution (1787) and the Bill of Rights (1789). The Constitution is not based on the Bible, but it was aware of its existence and made provision for its practice in at least one instance. "If any bill shall not be returned by the President within ten days (Sundays excepted) after it shall have been presented to him, the same shall be a law, in like manner as if he had signed it" (U.S. Constitution, Art. I, Section 7, Paragraph 2). The Constitution acknowledges Sunday, the Christian day of observance, not the Jewish Saturday nor the Muslim Friday. Moreover, fifty-two of the fifty-five signers of the Constitution were members of churches in the colonies.

The Bill of Rights At the 1954 Prayer Breakfast in Washington DC, Earl Warren (1891-1975), chief justice of the Supreme Court, said, "I believe no one can read the history of our country without realizing that the Good Book and the spirit of the Savior have from the beginning been our guiding geniuses.... I believe the entire Bill of Rights came into being because of the knowledge our forefathers had of the Bible and their express belief in it" (Warren, cited by Roger Schultz, "A Christian America: Earl Warren and Our Christian Roots," posted at https://chalcedon.edu/magazine/a-christian-america-earl-warren-and-our-christian-roots).

Congress In 1812, President James Madison signed a congressional bill that gave money to a Bible Society to distribute Bibles (*The Debates and Proceedings in the Congress of the United States*, 1853, p. 1325, cited by Barton, p. 215).

Leaders The Constitution does not require the president to take the oath of office by swearing on a Bible, but beginning with George Washington, all U.S. presidents have taken the oath of office with their hand on a Bible, except John Quincy Adams and Teddy Roosevelt. Adams was a religious man, but he chose to be sworn in with his hand on a book of U.S. laws to demonstrate that he recognized a barrier between church and state and that his loyalty was to our nation's laws above all else. Roosevelt's reason is unclear. Beyond swearing on the Bible, leaders said they recognized the need for the Bible in governing people and/or they respected the Bible.

Benjamin Franklin (1706-1790), a signer of the Declaration of Independence and the Constitution, said, "History will also afford frequent opportunities of showing the necessity of a public religion.... The excellency of the Christian religion above all others, ancient or modern" (Franklin, cited by Barton, p, 174), which is based on the Bible.

Thomas Jefferson (1743-1826), author of the Declaration of Independence and third President of the U.S., did not believe in the deity of Jesus Christ, but he said, "I am a real Christian, that is to say, a disciple of the doctrines of Jesus" (Jefferson, cited by Barton, p. 150).

James Madison (1751-1836) was the author of 29 of the 85 *Federalist Papers* and the fourth President of the U.S. (1809-1817). Because he was reticent to discuss his religious convictions, scholars debated exactly what his religious opinions were (for a detailed discussion, see Smith, pp. 51-58). Some depict him as a devoted evangelical, while others label him a Deist (Smith, p. 53). Frazer concludes he was a theistic rationalist (pp. 164-166). At any rate, Madison made copious notes in his Bible, and in Acts 19, he wrote, "Believers who are in a state of grace, have need of the word of God for their edification and building up, therefore, implies the possibility of falling. v. 32" (Madison, cited by Barton, p. 412).

John Jay (1745–1829) was a member of the First and Second Continental Congresses, one of the authors of the *Federalist Papers*, the first Chief Justice of the Supreme Court, and President of the American Bible Society. He said, "In forming and settling my belief relative to the doctrines of Christianity, I adopt no articles from creeds but such only as, on careful examination, I found to be confirmed by the Bible" (Jay, cited by Barton, p. 318; Federer, p. 318).

George Washington (1732-1799), the first President (1789-1797), is often quoted as saying in his "Farewell Address" (1796), "It is impossible to rightly govern the world without God and the Bible." That is not exactly what he said. The Farewell Address reads, "Of all the dispositions and habits which lead to political prosperity, religion, and morality are indispensable supports.... And let us with caution indulge the supposition that morality can be maintained without religion.... Reason and experience both forbid us to expect that national morality can prevail in the exclusion of religious principles. It is substantially true that virtue or morality is a necessary spring of popular government" (The "Farewell Address" is posted at www.americanyawp.com/reader/a-new-nation/george-washington-farewell-address-1796/). He is saying government must have morality and morality must have religion (he uses the word "indispensable"). In the context of his day, he is referring to Christianity and the Bible.

John Adams (1735-1826), the second President (1797-1801), was a Unitarian (Smith, p. 15). Yet, on February 22, 1756, he wrote in his diary, "Suppose a nation in some distant region should take the Bible for their only law book, and every member should regulate his conduct by the precepts there exhibited. Every member would be obliged in conscience to temperance and frugality and industry, to justice and kindness and charity towards his fellow men, and to piety and love, and reverence towards Almighty God…. What a Eutopia, what a Paradise would this region be" (https://founders.archives.gov/documents/Adams/01-01-02-0002-0002; Federer, p. 5).

John Quincy Adams (1767-1848), the sixth President (1825 to 1829), like his father, was a Unitarian (Smith, p. 92). In a letter to his son (1811), he wrote, "I have myself, for many years, made it a practice to read through the Bible once every year.... My custom is to read four or five chapters every morning immediately after rising from my bed. It employs about an hour of my time…. The Bible contains the revelation of the will of God" (Adams, cited by Federer, p. 16).

Harry Truman (1884-1972) was the 33rd President (1945-1953), said to the Attorney General's Conference in 1950, "The fundamental basis of this nation's laws was given to Moses on the Mount. The fundamental basis of our Bill of Rights comes from the teachings we get from Exodus and Saint Matthew, from Isaiah and Saint Paul. I don't think we emphasize that enough these days. If we don't have a proper fundamental moral background, we will finally end up with a totalitarian government that does not believe in rights for anybody except the State!" (Federer, p. 21).

Ronald Reagan (1911-2004), the 40th President (1981-1989), declared, "Of the many influences that have shaped the U.S. into a distinctive nation and people, none may be said to be more fundamental and enduring than the Bible" (posted at the Ronald Reagan Foundation and Institute, https://www.reaganfoundation.org/, quote #4548). He also said, "Inside the Bible's pages lie all the answers to all of the problems man has ever known… It is my firm belief that the enduring values presented in its pages have a great meaning for each of us and for our nation" (https://www.reaganfoundation.org/, quote #4043).

Some scholars have objected to these kinds of quotations, arguing that these were politicians and they were saying these things not because of their personal beliefs but because it was politically expedient. Even if that is true, it is evident that *the Bible heavily influenced society at the time*.

Conclusion The Bible greatly influenced the original U.S. *society*. The opening statement of National Geographic's 2018 edition of *Atlas of the Bible* says, "No other book has been a greater influence on the development of Western civilization than the Bible" (Jean-Pierre Isbouts, *Atlas of the Bible*, p. 5).

Kroll illustrates how the Bible has influenced American society by pointing out that if you drive west from Philadelphia, which is a name from the Bible (Rev. 3:7), within two hours, you can be in a number of cities having biblical names, such as Bethlehem, Nazareth, Emmaus, Bethany, Shiloh, Bethel, Eden, Zionsville, and new Jerusalem. You can also stop by Mount Nebo, Mount Zion, Lebanon, and Mount Carmel. And that's just Pennsylvania! You can visit Athens, Corinth, Palestine, Hebron, Eden, Joshua, and Corpus Christi in Texas. In California, you can go to Antioch, Carmel, Goshen, Bethel Island, Joshua Tree, Temple City, and Paradise (Kroll, pp. 37-38).

God Was Acknowledge

The Bible The Bible, of course, declares there is a God. Its opening statement is, "In the beginning, God created the heavens and the earth" (Genesis 1:1). In the early days of the U.S., the people and leaders either acknowledged the God of the Bible or, at least, acknowledged that there is a Creator. Most of the people and some of the leaders were Christians.

The People Benjamin Franklin told the French, "In America ... serious religion, under various denominations, is not only tolerated but it is also respected and practiced. Atheism is unknown there; infidelity [the rejection of Christianity] is rare and secret; so that person may live to a great age in that country, without having their piety shocked with either an atheist or an infidel" (Franklin, *Information to Those Who Would Remove to America*. London: M. Gunney, 1794, pp. 22-23, cited by Millard, p. 125 see also Barton, p. 140; Federer, p. 247). As was pointed out in the introduction, in 1776, when the Declaration of Independence was signed, approximately 98 percent of the colonists were Protestant Christians, 1.9 percent were Roman Catholics, and 2500 were Jews. "Calvinism was the prevailing theology in the previous century in America and remained the official theology of roughly two-thirds of American churches in the Founding era (Frazer, p. 116).

Declaration of Independence The Declaration of Independence not only speaks of "Nature's God." It declares, "We, therefore, the representatives of the United States of America, in General Congress assembled, appealing to the *Supreme Judge of the world* for the rectitude of our intentions, do, in the name, and by authority of the good people of these colonies, solemnly publish and declare that these United Colonies are, and of right ought to be, free and independent states; ... And for the support of this declaration, with a firm reliance on the protection of *divine Providence*, we mutually pledge to each other our lives, our fortunes, and our sacred honor" (Declaration of Independence, italics added). It also declares, "We hold these truths to be self-evident, that all men are created equal, that they are endowed by their *Creator* with unalienable rights, that among these are Life, Liberty and the pursuit of Happiness" (Declaration of Independence, italics added). The Declaration of Independence mentions God four times.

According to Petro, two-thirds of those who signed the Declaration of Independence were Anglicans (Petro). John Witherspoon (1723-1794), a Presbyterian pastor and president of New Jersey College (now Princeton University), was the only clergyman to sign the Declaration of Independence.

Charles Carroll (1737-1832), a delegate to the Continental Congress and Confederation Congress, delegate to the Continental Congress and Confederation Congress, was the lone Catholic to sign the Declaration of Independence.

Continental Congress During the Revolutionary War, open acknowledgment of reliance on God by civic leaders was a common practice. The Continental Congress issued proclamations for prayer, fasting, and thanksgiving 15 times during the Revolutionary War. In addition, literally scores of similar proclamations, often strongly and openly Christian, were issued by individual governors for their states, including John Hancock of Massachusetts, William Livingston of New Jersey, John Dickerson of Pennsylvania, and others (Barton, p. 116).

In October 1775, the Continental Congress established a Naval Committee. In November, the committee gave Congress a set of rules for the Navy entitled *Rules for the Regulation of the Navy of the United Colonies*. The *Rules* were basically the work of John Adams and were based on regulations for the British

Navy. "ART. 2. The Commanders of the ships of the Thirteen United Colonies are to take care that divine service be performed twice a day on board and a sermon preached on Sundays unless bad weather or other extraordinary accidents prevent it. ART. 3. If any shall be heard to swear, curse, or blaspheme the name of God, the Captain is strictly enjoined to punish them for every offense by causing them to wear a wooden collar or some other shameful badge of distinction, for so long a time as he shall judge proper" (see the entire *Rules* at https://www.navyhistory.org/rules-for-the-regulation-of-the-navy-of-the-united-colonies-of-north-america/).

Paris Peace Treaty (1783). The Peace Treaty ending the Revolutionary War begins with the words, "In the Name of the Most Holy & undivided Trinity. It having pleased the Divine Providence to dispose of the Hearts of...." (a copy of the Treaty of Paris is posted at https://www.ourdocuments.gov/doc.php?flash=false&doc=6&page=transcrip).

Constitution With a longhand version of dating rarely used today, the Constitution was signed on "the Seventeenth Day of September in *the Year of our Lord* one thousand seven hundred and Eighty-seven" (italics added).

The U.S. Government All three branches of the U.S. government (legislative, executive, and judicial) acknowledge God. Since 1777, every session of **Congress** begins with a prayer by a chaplain whose salary is paid by the taxpayers. In the Senate Chamber, an inscription over the south entrance reads "In God We Trust" and an inscription over the east doorway reads "*Annuit coeptis*" ("God has favored our undertakings"). From 1795 until well after the Civil War, weekly church services were continually held and attended by U.S. presidents, senators, and Republicans (see Barton, p. 125, who lists extensive documentation in a lengthy footnote). When our nation was attacked on September 11, 2001, the members of Congress spontaneously sang "God Bless America" on the steps of the Capitol building.

Since George Washington first added "so help me God" to his inaugural oath, every **president** since has likewise asked for God's assistance at his inauguration. On November 1, 1800, John Adams became the first U.S. President to move into the White House. One day later, he composed a prayer that is now inscribed on the mantelpiece in the State Dining Room: "I pray Heaven to bestow the best of blessings on this house and all that shall hereafter inhabit it. May none but honest and wise men ever rule under this roof."

Since at least the 1820s, the **Supreme Court** has opened its sessions with the prayer "God save the United States and this Honorable Court." Originally, the Supreme Court justices traveled to different locations across the country to impanel grand juries to hear cases rather than requiring all parties to travel to the federal capital. James Ken, one of the two Fathers of American Jurisprudence, observed that this was a practice with biblical precedents (1 Samuel 7:15-16). Prayer was a regular part of those sessions (Barton, pp. 123-124).

The U.S. Currency In a letter dated November 13, 1860, M. R. Watkinson, who identified himself as a minister of the gospel, asked the Secretary of the Treasury, S. P. Chase, to recognize Almighty God in some form on U.S. coins. In the letter, he also said, "This would make a beautiful coin to which no possible citizen could object," indicating how acknowledgment of God had impacted the current *society*. Chase sent a letter to the director of the men in Philadelphia in which he stated, "The trust of our people in God should be declared on our national coins." It took several years to finalize the motto. As a result, by an act of Congress on March 3, 1865, "In God we trust" was inscribed upon U.S. coins (Millard, pp.

380-381; see also the Department of Treasury website https://www.treasury.gov/about/education/Pages/in-god-we-trust.aspx).

The Pledge of Allegiance Abraham Lincoln closed the Gettysburg address, which took two minutes to deliver on November 19, 1863, with the words, "This nation, under God, shall have a new birth of freedom, and this government of the people, by the people, for the people shall not perish from the earth." He was the first U.S. president to use the expression "this nation under God." After his death, a "Lincoln Day of Observance Service" was held at the New York Avenue Presbyterian Church, two blocks from the White House. In 1954, Dwight Eisenhower and his wife attended that service. Eisenhower was so moved by George Docherty's sermon entitled "Under God," taken from Lincoln's words, that he initiated a proposal to have it permanently made a part of the Pledge of Allegiance (1954), which now reads "I pledge allegiance to the flag of the United States of America and to the Republic for which it stands, one nation under God, indivisible, with liberty and justice for all" (Millard, p. 167).

Days of Prayer and Thanksgiving On October 3, 1789, one week after Congress approved the Bill of Rights, George Washington spoke of "the duty of all Nations to acknowledge the providence of Almighty God, to obey his will, to be grateful for his benefits, and humbly to implore his protection and favor," and therefore declared a national "day of public thanksgiving and prayer to be observed by acknowledging with grateful hearts the many signal favors of Almighty God, especially by affording them an opportunity peaceably to establish a form of government for their safety and happiness." President Abraham Lincoln declared the last Thursday in November 1863, as "a day of thanksgiving and prayer to our beneficent Father who dwelleth in the heavens." Since then, all presidents have called on the nation annually to thank God in the Thanksgiving season.

Other aspects of the government acknowledge God. For example, the aluminum capstone that crowns the Washington Monument is inscribed on the east face with "LAUS DEO," Latin for "Praise be to God."

Leaders From the beginning and throughout the history of the U.S., political leaders have acknowledged God. In his book, *The Faiths of the Founding Fathers*, historian David L. Holmes divides the Founding Fathers into three religious categories: 1) The smallest group was Deists. Deists believed in a Creator who did not intervene in the universe. This group includes Thomas Paine and Ethan Allen. 2) Another group consisted of practicing Christians who believed in the deity of Jesus Christ. This group includes Patrick Henry, John Jay, and Samuel Adams. 3) The largest group retained Christian loyalties and practices but was influenced by Deism. People in all three categories believed in God.

Benjamin Franklin is said to be a Deist, but "Franklin defined his own Deism by five highly minimalistic principles: 1. That there is a God who made all things. 2. That he governs the world by his providence. 3. That he ought to be worshipped by adoration, prayer, and thanksgiving, but that the most acceptable service to God is doing good to man. 4. That the soul is immortal. 5. And that God will certainly reward virtue and punish vice, either here or hereafter" (Franklin, cited by Guelzo, p. 27; see also Franklin's letter to the President of Yale University, Federer, pp. 250-251). Unlike Deists, Franklin talked about God governing the world by His providence.

In his book *The Religious Beliefs of American Founders*, Frazer points out that in the quarter-century leading up to the revolution, roughly half of the books and pamphlets published in America discuss *politics* from a *religious* perspective (Frazer, p. 7).

He says, "The founders were religious men who believed religion was a critical support for free societies" (Frazer, p. 1). His analysis is that the *key founders* were not Christians in the biblical sense of the term, nor were they Deists. He calls their religion "theistic rationalism." Theistic rationalism is the belief that a benevolent creator God established laws, that He is active in human affairs, and that He hears and answers prayer. Theistic rationalism never became popular among the masses (Frazer, p. 22). Frazer discusses the theistic rationalism of Benjamin Franklin, Thomas Jefferson, James Madison, Alexander Hamilton, George Washington, John Adams, Gouverneur Morris, and James Wilson.

Of the first 46 presidents, 37 were Protestant, two were Catholic, and all believed in God. Eleven presidents were **Episcopalian**: George Washington, James Madison, James Monroe, William Harrison, John Tyler, Zachary Taylor, Franklin Pierce, Chester Arthur, Franklin Roosevelt, Gerald Ford, and George H. W. Bush. Nine presidents were **Presbyterian**: Andrew Jackson, James Polk, James Buchanan, Grover Cleveland, Benjamin Harrison, Woodrow Wilson, Dwight Eisenhower, Ronald Reagan, and Donald Trump. Four presidents have been **Baptist**: Warren Harding, Harry Truman, Jimmy Carter, and Bill Clinton; four have been **Methodist**: Ulysses Grant, Rutherford Hayes, William McKinley, and George W. Bush. Four have been **Unitarian**: John Adams, John Quincy Adams, Millard Fillmore, and William Howard Taft. Two were **Disciples of Christ**: James Garfield and Lyndon Johnson; two were **Dutch Reformed**: Martin Van Buren and Theodore Roosevelt and two were **Quakers**: Herbert Hoover and Richard Nixon. One was a **Congregationalist**: Calvin Coolidge; one was **United Church of Christ**: Barack Obama; and two were **Roman Catholic**: John F. Kennedy and Joe Biden. Three had **no formal affiliation**: Thomas

Jefferson, Abraham Lincoln (Lincoln planned to join a church, but he was killed a few days before he was scheduled to do that.), and Andrew Johnson, who identified himself as a Christian but never joined a church.

Thomas Jefferson was an Anglican. An article entitled "Jefferson's Religious Beliefs" from *The Thomas Jefferson Encyclopedia* says, "He was baptized and raised Anglican (and married and buried by Anglican ministers), but he rejected many of the tenets of that church.... Jefferson was a devout theist, believing in a benevolent creator God to whom humans owed praise. In an early political tract, he wrote, 'The God who gave us life gave us liberty at the same time.' ... In 1823, he wrote to John Adams referring to 'the God whom you and I acknowledge and adore' while denouncing atheism" (https://www.monticello.org/site/research-and-collections/jeffersons-religious-beliefs, accessed August 12, 2019).

James Madison, in his first inaugural address, spoke of "The guardianship and guidance of the Almighty whose power regulates the destiny of nations [and] whose blessings had been so conspicuously bestowed upon this rising Republic" (Madison, cited by Smith, p. 60).

Alexander Hamilton (1755 or 1757-1804), who was a member of the Continental Congress, a representative to the Constitutional Convention, a signer of the Constitution, author of 51 of 84 *Federalist Papers*, and the first Secretary of State, said, "I have carefully examined the evidences of the Christian religion, and if I were sitting as a juror upon its authenticity, I would unhesitatingly give my verdict in its favor.... I can prove its truth as clearly as any proposition ever submitted to the mind of man." His last words were: "I am a sinner. I have a tender reliance on the mercy of the Almighty, through the merits of the Lord Jesus Christ" (see the article by Mark Ellis, *The*

Faith of Alexander Hamilton, based on a biography of Hamilton written by Ron Chernow. The Ellis article is posted at https://godreports.com/2018/06/the-faith-of-alexander-hamilton/; see also Hamilton, cited by Barton, p. 274).

John Jay said, "The Bible will also inform them [the people] that our gracious Creator has provided for us a Redeemer ... that this Redeemer has made atonement 'for the sins of the whole world,' and thereby reconciling the divine justice with the divine mercy has opened the way for our redemption and salvation" (Federer, p. 318).

George Washington was an Episcopalian. Burk says. "Robert Lewis, Washington's nephew and private secretary, in 1827 told Mr. Sparks that he had accidentally witnessed his (Washington's) private devotions in his library, both morning and evening; that on one of these occasions, he had seen him in a kneeling position with the Bible open before him and that he believes such to have been a daily practice!" (Burk, cited by Millard, p. 70). John Marshall, who served with Washington at Valley Forge and later became the Chief Justice of the Supreme Court, said of Washington, "Without making ostentatious professions of religion, he was a sincere believer in the Christian faith and a truly devout man" (Marshall, cited by Federer, p. 417). After Washington's death, his well-worn, hand-written prayer book was found. The name "Jesus Christ" was used 20 times, and numerous references to Jesus occur using other terms such as "Jesus," "Lord Jesus," etc. (Barton, p. 286). D. James Kennedy argues that Washington was a Christian (see his video presentation at www.youtube.com/watch?v=Syz7Xa6dgDM). Frazer contends he was not (Frazer, p. 197). Whether or not Washington was a Christian, there is no doubt that he believed in God.

John Quincy Adams (1767-1848), the sixth President of the U.S., was a Unitarian, although he never explicitly denied the deity of Christ (Smith, p. 92). In a letter dated January 3, 1817, John Quincy Adams wrote, "My hopes of a future life are all founded upon the Gospel of Christ." He added that he could not quibble with Christ's disciples, "asserting that He was God" (Barton, p. 142).

Andrew Jackson (1767-1845) was the seventh President (1829-1837). "During his last days on earth, Jackson repeatedly professed his belief in Christ's substitutionary atonement and urged others to do the same" (Smith, p. 129).

Abraham Lincoln (1809-1865), the 16th President (1861-1865), on his departure from Springfield, Illinois to Washington (February 11, 1861), as President-elect, Lincoln said, "Without the assistance of the Divine Being who ever attended him, I cannot succeed. With that assistance, I cannot fail. Trusting in Him who can go with me, remain with you, and be everywhere for good, let us confidently hope that all will yet be well. To His care commending you, as I hope in your prayers, you will commend me, I bid you an affectionate farewell" (address posted at http://www.abrahamlincolnonline.org/lincoln/speeches/farewell.htm)

Conclusion When the United States was founded, God was acknowledged. Nearly everyone in 18th century America believed in a Creator God (Frazer, p. 167). As Benjamin Franklin pointed out, there were virtually no atheists or agnostics in the country at the time (see Franklin's statement above).

Evidence that originally, the U.S. society acknowledged God is the requirement that officeholders believe in God. "All 13 of the original American colonies required attestation of religious belief or affiliation—a religious oath—as a prerequisite for an individual to hold public office" (https://www.mtsu.edu/first-amendment/article/927/religious-oaths). Many states removed that requirement from their constitutions, but the Supreme Court invalidated that requirement for good in 1961.

The House Judiciary Committee declared, "Christianity ... was the religion of the founders of the republic and they expected it to remain the religion of their descendants" (B. F. Morris, *The Christian Life and the Character of the Civil Institutions in the United States*, 1864, p. 323, cited by Barton, p. 175).

People Believed in Moral Responsibility

The Bible The Bible wants people to be free. The Old Testament declares, "Proclaim liberty throughout all the land unto all the inhabitants thereof" (Leviticus 25:10). At the same time, the Bible insists on moral responsibility. The second half of the Ten Commandments forbids murder, adultery, stealing, and lying. Later, during the time of Ezekiel, a proverb circulating in Jerusalem said, "The fathers eat sour grapes and the children's teeth are set on edge." The inhabitants of Jerusalem were using it to claim that they were suffering because of the sins of their forefathers. They blamed others for their condition, refusing to take personal responsibility for their actions (Ezekiel 18:1-2). The Lord declared that the people were to no longer use that proverb (Ezekiel 18:3) because they cannot blame their sinfulness on their ancestors. The Lord says that those who sin shall die (Ezekiel 18:4). People are personally responsible for their actions.

Likewise, the New Testament declares, "Stand fast therefore in the liberty [from the Mosaic Law] by which Christ has made us free, and do not be entangled again with a yoke of bondage" (Galatians 5:1) and insists, "For each one shall bear his own load" (Galatians 6:5), meaning they are morally responsible.

The United States A case can be made that the essence of the United States is freedom. The Declaration of Independence was a declaration of freedom. It announced, "We hold these truths to be self-evident, that all men are created equal, that they are endowed by their Creator with certain inalienable [incapable of being alienated, cannot be taken away] rights, that among these are Life, Liberty, and the pursuit of Happiness." The First Amendment to the Constitution states, "Congress shall make no law respecting an establishment of religion, or prohibiting the free exercise thereof; or abridging the freedom of speech, or of the press; or the right of the people peaceably to assemble, and to petition the government for a redress of grievances." In the Bill of Rights, the first right is the guarantee of freedom, freedom of religion, speech, press, assembly, and petition.

At the same time, the Founding Fathers recognized that there must also be restraint for freedom to exist. Benjamin Franklin wrote, "Only a virtuous people are capable of freedom. As nations become corrupt and vicious, they have more need of masters" (Franklin, cited by Federer, p. 247). James Madison said, "religion [is] the basis and foundation of government" (Madison, cited by Federer, p. 410). Alexander Hamilton wrote to a friend, "I now offer you the outline of the plan that they have suggested. Let an association be formed to be denominated 'the Christian Constitutional Society, 'its objectivity first; the support of the Christian religion second; the support of the United States" (Hamilton, cited by Barton, p. 274).

George Washington recognized that morality cannot be maintained without religion. In his farewell address, he said, "Of all the dispositions and habits which lead to political prosperity, religion, and morality are indispensable supports." He also said, "And let us with caution indulge the supposition that morality can be maintained without religion.... Reason and experience both forbid us to expect that national morality can prevail to the exclusion of religious principle." "Religion and morality are the essential pillars of civil society."

John Adams said, "Our Constitution was made only for a moral and religious people. It is wholly inadequate to the government of any other" (Adams, Works, vol. IX, p. 416, cited by Barton, p. 188; religion was various versions of Protestant Christianity). In a speech to the military, he said, "We have no government armed with power capable of contending with human passions unbridled by morality and religion" (Adams, cited by Federer, p. 10).

John Jay said, "The most effective means of securing and continuance of our civil and religious liberties is always to remember with reverence and gratitude the source from which they flow" (Jay, cited by Barton, p. 188).

Gouverneur Morris (1752–1816), signer to the Articles of Confederation, author of the Preamble of the Constitution, and penman and signer of the Constitution, said, "For avoiding the extremes of despotism or anarchy ... the only ground of hope must be on the morals of the people" (The Diaries and Letters of Gouverneur Morris, p. 413, available online at Google books).

Personal freedom and moral responsibility go hand in hand. Without restraint, the freedom of speech tolerates slander. Without moral responsibility, freedom of the press degenerates into the publication of propaganda. For freedom to prevail, there must be moral responsibility. In any society, there is either self-control, government control, or no control (chaos).

Furthermore, the U.S. moral ideals have their antecedent in Christian values. These values include truth, righteousness (as based on the Ten Commandments), justice, integrity, honesty, generosity, patience, love, mercy, compassion, etc. Dennis Prager argues that "Judeo-Christian values, right and wrong, good and evil, are derived from God, not from reason alone, nor from the human heart, the state, or through majority rule.... If there is no transcendent source of morality ... 'good' and 'evil' are subjective opinions, not objective realities" (Prager, "The Case for Judeo-Christian Values IV").

Horowitz, a Jewish agnostic, states, "As Christians, the American founders believed in free will—the responsibility of individuals for their actions and the result of their actions. Free will is what makes us equal, so long as government does not restrict our freedom. Recognizing that individuals make choices that affect their destinies, puts the responsibility for overcoming the handicaps of circumstances squarely on individual shoulders. This is a liberating idea. It is why America's inspirational stories are always stories about the triumph of the underdog, the ability of individuals to overcome their circumstances, to rise above their allotted stations in life, to achieve something better. For over 200 years, that vision has been the American dream" (Horowitz, p. 141).

After touring the U.S., a French historian and social philosopher, Alexis de Tocqueville (1805-1859), wrote the two-volume *Democracy in America* (1835 and 1840). He observed, "All sects [denominations] increase the same moral law in the name of God.... Moreover, all sects of the United States are comprised within the greater unity of Christianity and Christian morality is everywhere the same.... There is no country in the world where the Christian religion retains a greater influence over the souls of men than in America.... The Americans combine the notions of Christianity and of liberty so intricately in their minds that it is impossible to make them conceive of one without the other" (Tocqueville, cited by Federer, pp. 204-205).

Conclusion From the beginning, the people of the U.S. believed in freedom, but they were also taught biblical values at home and later in the school system. See the next two sections on family and education.

The Traditional Family Was The Norm

The Bible One of the results of respecting the Bible is the traditional family. When Adam and Eve were still in the Garden, God said, "A man shall leave his father and mother and be joined to his wife" (Genesis 2:24). Neither Adam nor Eve had a father or mother! From the very beginning, God established that there was to be marriage and family. Marriage consists of leaving parents to establish a new family unit. The new family unit was to have children (Genesis 1:28) and when they did, they were to teach them the Word of God (Deuteronomy 6:7; Ephesians 6:4). In the Ten Commandments, sandwiched between people's relationship to God (the first four Commandments) and their relationship to one another (Commandments six through nine) the fifth commandment is "Honor your father and mother" (Exodus 20:12).

From a biblical perspective, the immediate family is primarily responsible for rearing children, but grandparents also influence their grandchildren. Grandparents are to tell their grandchildren what they have seen the Lord do (Exodus 10:1-2). They must also teach their grandchildren the Word of God (Deuteronomy 4:9-10). Timothy knew the Scriptures from childhood (2 Timothy 3:15) because of the impact of the faith of his grandmother Lois and his mother Eunice (2 Timothy 1:5). Ideally, if everyone followed God's instructions concerning the family, all children would have six adults, two parents and two sets of grandparents, who loved them, encouraged them, and supported them.

Virtues such as respect for authority and personal responsibility were ingrained in children by their parents, neighbors, teachers, and pastors so that by the time they reached adulthood, respect and responsibility were part and parcel of their character.

The United States Remember that in 1776, 98% of the people in the colonies were Protestant Christians. Thus, society at large was well aware of the fifth commandment. In 1835, Tocqueville wrote that the influence of religious faith "over the mind of women is supreme and women are the protectors of morals. There is certainly no country in the world where the tie of marriage is more respected than in America or where the conjugal happiness is more highly or worthily appreciated" (Tocqueville, cited by Federer, p. 205). Benjamin Harrison (1833-1901), the 23rd President (1889-1893), said the American family was taken from the Sacred Book.

As a nation, "we began with the model of a rational and industrial man, who was honest, respected laws, and was dedicated to the family (his own family—what has in its decay been dubbed the nuclear family). Above all, he was to know the rights doctrine, the Constitution, which embodied it; and American history, which presented and celebrated the founding of a nation 'conceived in liberty and dedicated to the proposition that all men are created equal'" (Bloom, pp. 26-27).

Ronald Reagan wrote, "The family has always been the cornerstone of American society. Our families nurture, preserve, and pass on to each succeeding generation the values we share and cherish, values that are foundational to our freedoms. In the family, we learn our first lessons of God and man, love and discipline, rights and responsibilities, human dignity, and human frailty. Our families give us daily examples of those lessons being put into practice. In raising and instructing our children, and providing personal and compassionate care for the elderly, and maintaining the spiritual strength of religious commitment among our people—in these and other ways, American families make immeasurable contributions to American well-being. Today more than ever, it is essential that these contributions not be taken for granted and that each of us remember that the strength of our families is vital to the strength of our nation" (Reagan, cited by Federer, p. 531).

The "dissolution of marriage" was considered to be against the public interest and was frowned upon in society, no doubt, because of the influence of Christianity and the Bible. Until the 21st century, marriage in this country was what marriage had always been throughout the entire history of the human race: a marriage between a man and a woman.

Christianity Influenced Education

The Bible According to the Bible, the family has the first and foremost responsibility for teaching the Scripture (Deuteronomy 6:6-9).

Elementary Education In the colonies, from the beginning, children were homeschooled or sent to schools organized by parents, towns, and churches. Some were educated through work apprenticeships. The first public school was the Boston Latin School, founded in 1635.

Between 1687 and 1690, *The New England Primer*, based on *The Protestant Tutor* that had been published in England, was published in Boston. It was the first reading primer designed for the

American Colonies. The content of *The New England Primer* varied over time, although the standard material for beginning reading instruction included the alphabet, vowels, consonants, double letters, and syllabaries of two letters to six-letter syllables. The 90-page work contained religious maxims, catechism answers, and moral lessons. It was filled with Calvinist theology. Many of its selections were drawn from the King James Bible. Scholars estimate that two to three million copies of the primer were sold over the course of 150 years. The widespread use of *The New England Primer* indicates that the Bible was deeply embedded in American education.

"During the first 150 years [1620-1770] in the English colonies, [many] children were homeschooled. Parents took seriously their role to teach their children how to read, write, cipher [math], and cultivate virtuous character and Christian conscience for the future citizenry. The Bible was their primer, and children were catechized. John Locke characterized the reading curriculum of the American colonies as 'the ordinary road of Hornbook, Primer, Psalter, Testament, and Bible.' After home education, many colonial boys attended grammar school and were taught Latin, the language of scholarship, by their local pastor" (Elizabeth Youmans; see bibliography).

The founding fathers believed education was essential for the new republic's survival. Thomas Jefferson, John Adams, and others supported establishing publicly funded schools. In 1779, Jefferson submitted a proposal to the Virginia legislature to create free elementary schools throughout the state, regardless of family income. Not wanting to assume the burden of educating the poor, the bill was defeated. In 1785, the Continental Congress adopted the Land Ordinance. It reserved a portion of revenues from land sales to fund public schools in the states carved out of the Northwest

Territory (https://files.eric.ed.gov/fulltext/ED503799.pdf).

Benjamin Rush (1746-1813), a signer of the Declaration of Independence, said, *"The only foundation for a useful education in a republic is to be an aid in religion. Without this, there can be no virtue, and without virtue, there can be no liberty, and liberty is the object and life of all republican governments"* (Rush, *Essays, Literary, Moral and Philosophical,* 1798, p. 8, cited by Barton, p. 159, italics his). He also said, "Without religion, I believe that learning does real mischief to the morals and principles of mankind" (Rush, Letters of Benjamin, vol. I, p. 294, cited by Barton, p. 159).

Gouverneur Morris (1752–1816), signer to the Articles of Confederation, author of the Preamble of the Constitution, and penman and signer of the Constitution, said, "Religion is the only solid basis for good morals; therefore education should teach the precepts of religion and duties of man towards God" (Jared Sparks, *The Life of Gouverneur Morris,* 1832, vol. III, p. 483, cited by Barton, p. 159; Federer, p. 455).

Fisher Ames (1758-1808), who provided the final wording for the First Amendment, called for "the Bible [to] always remain the principal textbook in American classrooms" (Ames, *Works of Fisher Ames,* 1809, pp. 134-135, cited by Barton, p. 218).

When George Washington signed the Northwest Ordinance (August 7, 1789), he encouraged schools in the territory that would become Illinois to teach "religion, morality, and knowledge" ("An Ordinance of the Territory of the United States Northwest of the River Ohio," Article III, cited by Barton, p. 158). At the invitation of Congress, chiefs from the Delaware Indian tribe brought three young Indians to George Washington to be trained in American schools. Commending them for their decision, Washington told them, "You do well to wish to learn our arts and ways of life and above all the religion of Jesus Christ" (Washington, *Writings,* vol. XV, p. 55, cited by Barton, p. 91).

Joseph Story (1779-1845), U.S. Supreme Court Justice and Father of American Jurisprudence said, "Why may not the Bible, especially the New Testament, without note or comment, be read and taught as divine revelation in the college—its general precepts expounded, its evidence explained in its glorious principles of morality inculcated? ... Where can the purest principles of morality be learned so clearly or perfectly from the New Testament?" (Story, cited by Barton, p. 160).

The New England Primer, first printed in 1687, was widely popular until it was supplanted by Noah Webster's *Blue Back Speller,* the most common textbook from 1790 until 1836. *The McGuffey Readers* appeared in 1836.

William Holmes McGuffey (1800-1873) was a college professor, a college president, and an ordained Presbyterian minister. He was passionate about preaching the gospel and instilling Calvinism in children through his books, emphasizing spelling, vocabulary, and formal public speaking. In 1836, McGuffey began producing *McGuffey's Readers* for grades 1-6, which "had a profound influence on American education" (Kroll, p. 30) because they were so widely used as textbooks for elementary schools from the mid-19th century to the mid-20th century. Between 1836 and 1960, 120 million copies of *McGuffey's Reader* were sold (see the article at https://www.nps.gov/jeff/learn/historyculture/upload/mcguffey.pdf)

The content changed between the 1836 edition and the 1879 edition. Salvation, righteousness, and piety were excluded from the later versions. Although his name appeared in later versions, McGuffey did not contribute to or approve their content. Henry Ford said that

McGuffey's Readers were one of the most important influences in his childhood. He paid for all six of the 1867 edition to be distributed to schools across the U.S.

In the 1830s, Horace Mann (1796-1859), secretary of the Massachusetts Board of Education, promoted "common school." These schools would be publicly funded, locally governed, and offer all students a common curriculum. Mann and other common-school reformers believed that "public schools would transform children into moral, literate, and productive citizens; eliminate poverty and crime; quell class conflict; and unify a population that was becoming more ethnically diverse" (https://files.eric.ed.gov/fulltext/ED503799.pdf). Historian Ellwood P. Cubberley said, "No one did more than he [Horace Mann] to establish in the minds of the American people the conception that education should be universal, non-sectarian, free, and that its aims should be social efficiency, civic virtue, and character, rather than mere learning or the advancement of sectarian ends."

The establishment of common schools was gradual. In 1852, Massachusetts became the first state to enact a compulsory education law. It required every city and town to offer primary school, focusing on grammar and basic arithmetic. They took over many of the educational tasks traditionally handled by parents. By the 1850s, many Northeastern and Midwestern states had free public education. However, it was not until the late 1900s that public elementary schools were available to all children in nearly all parts of the country. In the 1830s, about 55% of children 5 to 14 were enrolled in public schools. By 1870, 78% were enrolled. By 1918, all states required children to at least complete elementary school.

High Schools The first "secondary school" (high school) in the U.S. was founded in 1821 in Boston, Massachusetts. The Central

High School of Philadelphia, founded in 1830, was the second public high school. Six years later, the third high school was started in Baltimore, Maryland. It was named "The High School." In 1910, only 18% of those 15 to 18 years old were enrolled in high school. Barely 9% of 18-year-olds graduated from high school. From 1910 to 1940, the number of high schools rapidly multiplied. It is called the "high school movement." By 1940, 73% of the youths in America were enrolled in high school.

Higher Education Originally, Christians established colleges to train men for the ministry. Harvard, the oldest institution of higher learning in the U.S., was founded in 1636 to train men for the ministry. In 1639, it was renamed Harvard College after clergyman John Harvard, who willed the school money and his library of some 400 books. In 1701, the "Collegiate School," later renamed Yale in recognition of a gift from Elihu Yale, was established by Puritan clergy to educate Congregational ministers. In 1746, Presbyterians founded the College of New Jersey, later renamed Princeton University, to train ministers. Also, in 1746, the Anglicans set up Kings College in New York City, now known as Columbia University. In 1764, a group of Baptist leaders established Rhode Island College, renamed Brown University, in honor of a benefactor in 1804. In 1769, Dartmouth was founded by Eleazar Wheelock, a Congregational minister. Although he sought to establish a school to train Native Americans as Christian missionaries, Dartmouth primarily trained Congregationalist ministers throughout its early history.

In 1795, Timothy Dwight (1752-1817), Jonathan Edwards's grandson, became Yale's president. In 1802, about one-third of the students were converted due to his lectures and chapel sermons. (In 1802, Yale had 230 students.) From Yale, the revival spread to Dartmouth and other colleges.

In other words, higher education in the U.S. was largely provided in the colleges of the different religious denominations rather than the state. Of the 246 colleges founded by the close of 1860, 17 were state institutions and only two or three others had any state connections (Barton, p. 91).

Conclusion Initially, public schools focused on religion, family, and morality. The U.S. Constitution did not give the federal government authority over education. Education is not even mentioned in the Constitution.

Captialism was the Economic System

The Bible The Bible supports certain aspects of capitalism, such as the private ownership of property. The Ten Commandments say, "Do not steal" (Exodus 20:15). Commenting on this commandment, Dennis Prager said, "It has been shown over and over that private property, beginning with land ownership, is indispensable to creating a free and decent society. Every totalitarian regime takes away private property rights" (Prager, "The Ten Commandments," posted at prageruniversity.com). The private ownership of property is an essential part of capitalism.

The Bible sanctions the accumulation of wealth. While it warns the wealthy about the temptation of trusting in riches (1 Timothy 6:17-19), it also contains illustrations of very wealthy individuals, including Abraham, Solomon, and Barnabas. There is also an illustration of believers at Jerusalem having "all things in common" by selling their goods and possessions and dividing them among all as every one had need (Acts 2:45). That was not communism because it was done voluntarily, not by government mandate. And apparently, it did not work. Paul took free will offerings from the Gentile churches for the poor saints of Jerusalem (Romans 15:25-26). The accumulation of individual wealth is the essence of capitalism and the opposite of socialism.

The Bible sustains the idea of investing money to make money. In the parable of the talents, Jesus told of a man who gave three servants talents, a form of money, in Jesus' day. The first doubled his master's five talents through trading (Matthew 25:16). The second, who was given two talents, also doubled his master's money (Mathew 25:17). But the third buried his master's money (Mathew 25:18). In the parable, the master commended the first two and reprimanded the third, telling him, "You ought to have deposited my money with the bankers" so that you would've made "interest" (Mathew 25:27). Investing money to make money is the essence of capitalism.

Capitalism The economic system called capitalism is based on the private ownership of property (tangible assets such as land and houses and intangible assets such as stocks and bonds), private control of the production by individuals or companies for profit, competition, and the accumulation of capital. Capitalism is characterized by a free market for goods and services, an individual's choice of what to consume, and goods and services produced based on demand, which creates incentives to cut costs. Capitalism allows for self-interest (think "mutual benefit"); people with capital can pursue their own good without regard for sociopolitical pressure. The government plays a secondary role.

Capitalism developed during the 16th and 17th centuries in the Protestant countries of Northwestern Europe, especially in the Netherlands and England. Traders in Amsterdam and London created the first stock companies and the first stock exchange. Banking and insurance institutions were also established. None of this was called capitalism at the time. According to the *Oxford English Dictionary*, the term capitalism was first used by novelist William Makepeace Thackeray in 1854. He used the term to mean "having ownership of capital."

Adam Smith (1723-1790) is the father of modern capitalism theory. In 1776, he published *An Inquiry into the Nature and Causes of the Wealth of Nations*, usually called *The Wealth of Nations*. *The Wealth of Nations* was a precursor to the modern academic discipline of economics and laid the foundations of classical free-market economic theory. Smith's "invisible hand" concept is that, free of government regulations, a nation's economy would regulate itself and produce maximum efficiency. Motivated by rational self-interest to produce personal profit, as an unintended consequence, this "free market" system would maximize society's wealth. Rational self-interest and competition lead to economic prosperity. Tax preferences, monopolies, and lobbying threaten this system. Government should be limited to defense, public works, and the administration of justice, financed by taxes based on income.

Smith also recommended universal public schooling at government expense so that all and society could acquire the skills of reading, writing, and arithmetic (Muller, p. 37). In addition, Smith thought that a "commercial society," his term for capitalism, which wasn't coined until years later, would produce desirable character traits such as organization, frugality, concentration, honesty, and punctuality (see Muller, p. 40) and that a well-functioning market that led to greater prosperity was more likely to make people act more benevolently (Muller, p. 39).

At its founding, the United States was primarily an agricultural country with plantations in the South and some manufacturing in the

North (Muller, p. 57). Jefferson argued for an agrarian-based economy (he even thought that it was only in a society of small farmers that virtues could flourish (MacIntyre, p. 195), but Alexander Hamilton, who basically agreed with Adam Smith, supported a strong manufacturing economy. Hamilton wanted a more industrial republic because 1) manufacturing was more likely to result in a productive economy, 2) manufacturing left more room for enterprise (entrepreneurship), which would lead to a more productive society, 3) manufacturing would utilize a wider range of human abilities, 4) manufacturing would attract a wider range of people (immigrants), which the underpopulated country needed, 5) manufacturing would make farmers more productive, 6) manufacturing would be needed to produce the full range of commodities people needed during a time of war (Muller, pp. 57-58). Hamilton also wanted the government to spend money on infrastructure to provide the roads that made commerce possible and he recommended the creation of a national bank, which would have the power to issue paper money (Muller, p. 58). He put "manufacturing and money-lending in the driver's seat of the economy" (Guelzo, p. 33). When Thomas Jefferson founded the University of Virginia (1819), Adam Smith's book, *The Wealth of Nations*, was incorporated into the curriculum (Muller, Lecture 10).

The Industrial Revolution occurred over a century ago, with production moving from handmade goods in-home businesses to machine-aided factory production. In 1790, Elias Howe and Englishman Thomas Saint invented the sewing machine. In 1793, Samuel Slater (1768-1835), the "Father of the American Industrial Revolution" and the "Father of the American Factory System," opened a textile manufacturing mill in Pawtucket, Rhode Island and in 1812, built the Old Green Mill in Webster, Massachusetts. In 1807, Robert Fulton (1765-1815) developed a commercially successful steamboat service on the Hudson River between New York City and Albany. The War of 1812 demonstrated the need for the U.S. to further develop manufacturing (Muller, p. 58). In 1832, while returning from Europe, Morse met Charles Thomas Jackson, who was well-schooled in electromagnetism. As a result of that encounter, Morse developed the concept of a single-wire telegraph. By 1840, the U.S. was an international industrial powerhouse (Muller, pp 58-59). In 1869, the first transcontinental railroad was completed. In the meantime, between 1860 and 1900, 14 million immigrants came to the U.S., providing workers for various industries (https://www.loc.gov/classroom-materials/industrial-revolution-in-the-united-stat/).

Andrew Puzder, a Senior Fellow at Pepperdine University's School of Public Policy and former CEO of CKE Restaurant Holdings (Carl's Jr. and Hardee's restaurants), said, "America's wise founders took [Adam] Smith's principles to heart and within a mere 100 years—the blink of an eye historically—capitalism turned the United States from thirteen backwoods colonies into the world's largest economy. And it has held that position ever since" (Puzder, "The Market Will Set You Free," https://www.prageru.com/video/the-market-will-set-you-free/).

Conclusion The basic elements of capitalism, the private ownership of property, the accumulation of wealth, and using money to make money, were present in the U.S. when it was founded. In 1776, only a handful of corporations existed in the U.S., but corporations were integral to the economy by the middle of the nineteenth century.

The Rule of Law was the Rule

The Bible The rule of law is defined as "a principle under which all persons, institutions, and entities are accountable to laws that are publicly promulgated, equally enforced, independently adjudicated and consistent with international human rights principles" (see the article at https://www.uscourts.gov/educational-resources/educational-activities/overview-rule-law). The *Oxford English Dictionary* defines the rule of law as "the principle whereby all members of a society (including those in government) are considered equally subject to publicly disclosed legal codes and processes." In other words, everyone is under the law; no one is above the law. The rule of law also includes the concepts that people are innocent until proven guilty and due process. All of these legal principles are rooted in the Scripture, which influenced their implementation in modern times.

The principle of the rule of law is in the Bible. "Then I commanded your judges at that time, saying, 'Hear the cases between your brethren and judge righteously between a man and his brother or the stranger who is with him. You shall not show partiality in judgment; you shall hear the small as well as the great; you shall not be afraid in any man's presence, for the judgment is God's. The case that is too hard for you bring to me, and I will hear it'" (Deuteronomy 1:16-17). "You shall do no injustice in judgment. You shall not be partial to the poor nor honor the person of the mighty. In righteousness, you shall judge your neighbor" (Leviticus 19:15). Peter said, "In truth, I perceive that God shows no partiality" (Acts 10:34).

In Deuteronomy, God also said that the king should have a copy of the Law of Moses and read it all the days of his life that he might observe to do it. The king was not to multiply horses, wives, nor silver and gold for himself (Deuteronomy 17:16-19). In other words, the king was subject to the law, just like everyone else. By contrast, in ancient Greece, Plato advocated rule by a philosopher-king who was above the law.

The principle of innocent until proven guilty is in the Bible. "One witness shall not rise against a man concerning any iniquity or any sin that he commits; by the mouth of two or three witnesses, the matter shall be established" (Deuteronomy 19:15).

The principle of due process is in the Bible. "If a false witness rises against any man to testify against him of wrongdoing, then both men in the controversy shall stand before the LORD, before the priests and the judges who serve in those days. And the judges shall make careful inquiry, and indeed, *if* the witness *is* a false witness, who has testified falsely against his brother, then you shall do to him as he thought to have done to his brother; so you shall put away the evil from among you. And those who remain shall hear and fear, and hereafter they shall not again commit such evil among you" (Deuteronomy 19:16-20).

Magna Carta (1215) In the 13th century, after years of heavy taxation, England's King John was facing the possibility of a rebellion by the country's powerful barons. Stephen Langton (ca. 1150-1228), the Archbishop of Canterbury, drafted a charter of liberties known as the Magna Carta that placed King John and all future kings under the rule of law. It also promised the protection of church rights, the protection of the barons from illegal imprisonment, access to swift justice, and the limitation of feudal payments to the Crown.

The concept of due process is in the Magna Carta. Clause 39 states, "No free man shall be seized or imprisoned, or stripped of his rights or possessions, or outlawed or exiled, or deprived of his standing in any other way, nor will we proceed with force against him, or send others to do so, except by the lawful judgment of his equals or by the law of the land."

The phrase "due process" first appeared in a statutory rendition of Clause 39 in 1354. It stated, "No man of what state or condition he be, shall be put out of his lands or tenements nor taken, nor disinherited, nor put to death, without he be brought to answer by due process of law."

Divine Right of Kings The divine right of kings is defined as "The doctrine that monarchy is God's chosen form of government and that rebellion against the monarch is always a sin. Where active obedience to an evil ruler is morally impossible, it is held that passive obedience (i.e., willing acceptance of any penalty imposed for non-compliance) is demanded" (see the article at https://www.oxfordreference.com/view/10.1093/oi/authority.20110810104754564).

In the 16th century, Bishop John Ponet (ca. 1514-1556) opposed the divine right of kings to rule. He wrote *Shorte Treatise of Politike Power* (1556), proposing a radical resistance theory based on biblical examples. In the 17th century, the Scottish theologian Samuel Rutherford (ca. 1600-1661) employed it in arguing against the divine right of kings. John Locke (1632-1704) wrote that freedom in society means being subject only to laws made by a legislature that apply to everyone.

To sum up, in the 13th century, an archbishop drafted the Magna Carta, and in the 16th century, a bishop opposed the divine right of kings and wrote a book based on biblical examples that were expanded by John Locke, who influenced the Founding Fathers of the U.S. "Our legal system stems from a long European tradition that began with the Bible" (Bruce, p. 265).

Constitution The concept that a person is "innocent until proven guilty" is in the Constitution. "No person shall be convicted of treason unless on the testimony of two witnesses to the same overt act, or confession in open court" (U.S. Constitution, Art. III, Section 3, Paragraph 1). Due process is in the Constitution. The Fifth Amendment reads: "No person shall ... be deprived of life, liberty, or property, without due process of law." The Fourteenth Amendment says: "Nor shall any State deprive any person of life, liberty, or property, without due process of law."

Thomas Paine (1737-1809) On January 10, 1776, Thomas Paine published *Common Sense*, writing, "But where, say some, is the King of America? I'll tell you, Friend, he reigns above.... Let a day be solemnly set apart for proclaiming the charter; let it be brought forth placed on the divine law, the word of God; let a crown be placed thereon, by which the world may know, that so far as we approve as monarchy, that in America THE LAW IS KING. As in absolute governments, the King is law, so in free countries, the law ought to be King; and there ought to be no other" (https://www.ushistory.org/paine/commonsense/sense4.htm).

William Blackstone (1723-1780) William Blackstone, an English judge, wrote *Commentaries on the Laws of England*, which dominated the legal system for more than a century. His words shaped the Declaration of Independence, the Constitution, and the fundamental laws of the U.S. Blackstone wrote, "These laws laid down by God are the eternal, immutable laws of good and evil.... This law of nature dictated by God himself is, of course, superior in obligation to any other. It is binding over all the globe, in all countries, and at all times: no human laws are of any validity if contrary to this.... The doctrines thus delivered we call the revealed or divine law, and they are to be found only in the holy scriptures ... [and] are found upon comparison to be really part of the original law of nature. Upon these two foundations, the law of nature and the law of revelation, depend all human laws; that is to say, no human laws should be suffered to contradict these" (Blackstone, cited by Federer, p. 52)

Other aspects of the American judicial system are rooted in the Scripture. For example, compare "If a man makes a vow to the Lord, or swears an oath to bind himself by some agreement, he shall not break his word; he shall do according to all that proceeds out of his mouth" (Numbers 30:2) with "No state shall pass any law impairing the obligation of contracts." (U.S. Constitution, Art. I, Section 10, Paragraph 1)

The American judicial system is based on the Old Testament concept of justice. The Scripture says, "Your eye shall not pity: life *shall be* for life, eye for eye, tooth for tooth, hand for hand, foot for foot" (Deuteronomy 19:21). Other systems of justice are not like this; for example, in some applications of Muslim Sharia Law, stealing is punished by the amputation of a hand. In biblical justice, the punishment is commensurate with the crime. The words "equal justice under law" are written above the main entrance to the Supreme Court building.

Thr Sanctity of Life Accepted

The Bible The phrase "sanctity of life" expresses the idea that since humans are created in the image of God (Genesis 1:26-27), all human life is sacred. In the abortion debate, it is used of the concept that the fetus is a human life. (Abortion has been around for a long time. The first record of induced abortion is from the Egyptians in 1550 BC.) The Bible indicates that a fetus is a human being. For example, God is involved in conception: "When the Lord saw that Leah was unloved, He opened her womb; but Rachel was barren" (Genesis 29:31); "Then God remembered Rachel, and God listened to her and opened her womb" (Genesis 30:22; see also Ruth 4:13).

Furthermore, God is involved in the process of fashioning the fetus: "Your hands have made me and fashioned me, an intricate unity; yet You would destroy me. Remember, I pray that You have made me like clay. And will You turn me into dust again? Did you not pour me out like milk, and curdle me like cheese, clothe me with skin and flesh, and knit me together with bones and sinews?" (Job 10:8-11; see also Psalm 139:13-16). The Lord told Jeremiah, "Before I formed you in the womb, I knew you; before you were born, I sanctified you" (Jeremiah 1:5).

When Mary greeted Elizabeth, who was carrying John the Baptist in her womb, Elizabeth said, "the baby in my womb" leaped for joy (Luke 1:44). Leaping for joy is the function of a human being, not just part of a woman's body. The Greek word for "baby" means "an unborn child, a newborn child, a baby, an infant" (Abbott Smith Greek Lexicon). It is the same Greek word that is used to describe Jesus in the manger (Luke 2:16) and to describe Timothy as a child (2 Timothy 3:15). In other words, the Bible does not make a distinction between the human being before or after its birth.

The question is, "When does the fetus become human?" Is it at conception or sometime after that? David said, "Behold, I was brought forth in iniquity and in sin my mother conceived me" (Ps. 51:5). He was not saying his mother was in sin when he was conceived; he is saying he was a sinner from conception.

Some Christians have argued that Exodus 21:22-24 indicates that God does not regard the fetus as human because it says if a man strives with a pregnant woman, causing her to have a miscarriage, the destruction of the fetus is not a capital offense. Therefore, the fetus, it is argued, is not human. Others insist Exodus 21:22 is not talking about a miscarriage. It refers to the premature birth of an otherwise healthy child, which is the way it is translated in the NKJV, NASB 1995, and the NIV. The Hebrew verb translated "give birth prematurely" is never used to indicate a miscarriage. Another Hebrew word, *shachel*, is used for miscarriage (Exodus 23:26).

Exodus 21:22 teaches that the guilty party is fined if there is a premature birth or no other harm is done. On the other hand, if there is further harm to either the mother or the child, then the assailant must pay an eye for an eye, life for life (Exodus 21:23). So, this passage is not talking about miscarriage; it is distinguishing between a premature birth in which neither the mother nor the child is harmed and the premature birth when one or the other is injured or dies. In the latter case, the life of the fetus is valued just as highly as the life of the mother. Therefore, if the fetus is a human being from conception, aborting the fetus is killing a human being.

Church History From the first century, the position of the Christian church has been that the fetus is a human life. The *Didache*, which was written either before 100 AD or early in the second century, declares, "You shall not murder a child by abortion nor kill them when born" (*Didache* 2:2; https://legacyicons.com/content/didache.pdf, p. 5). *The Epistle of Barnabas* (130 AD) says, "You shall not slay the child by procuring abortion~ nor, again, shall you destroy it after it is born" (https://conciliarpost.com/wp-content/uploads/2016/05/TheEpistleofBarnabas.pdf). These are two examples of the virtually unanimous testimony of the early church in opposition to abortion (see https://vitalsignsministries.org/articles_posts/views-on-abortion-from-church-history/).

Here are a few more examples. The early Christian author Tertullian (160-220 AD) wrote, "With them [Christians] it is utterly unlawful to take away a child in the womb when nature is in deliberation about the man; for to kill a child before it is born is to commit murder by way of advance; and there is no difference whether you destroy a child in its formation, or after it is formed and delivered. For we Christians look upon him as a man, who is one in embryo; for he is in being, like the fruit in blossom, and in a little time would have been a perfect man, had nature met with no disturbance" (http://www.tertullian.org/articles/reeve_apology.htm).

Theologian Jerome (347-420 AD) wrote, "Some [unmarried women] even ensure barrenness by the help of potions, murdering human beings before they are fully conceived. Others, when they find that they are with child as the result of their sin, practice abortion with drugs and so frequently bring about their own death, taking with them to the lower world the guilt of three crimes: suicide, adultery against Christ, and child murder" (Jerome, *Letter to Eustochium*; posted at https://epistolae.ctl.columbia.edu/letter/447.html).

The early church father John Chrysostom (about 347-407 AD) speaks about "murder before the birth" and making "the chamber of procreation a chamber for murder" (Chrysostom, Homily 24 on Romans; https://www.newadvent.org/fathers/210224.htm).

The view of Augustine (354-430) was more complex. As one author explains, "It is commonly known that Augustine followed the tradition of Aristotle in that he considered the progression of life in the womb to begin with a vegetative or plant-like existence and soul, then an animal soul, and finally a human soul with (according to Augustine) the complete moral value of a human being. Though Augustine's writings indicate he struggled over the idea of delayed humanization or ensoulment, Augustine chose not to delve too deeply into when exactly this occurred and whether the embryo should be considered a valuable human entity from the moment of conception…. He did make it clear, however, that abortion at any stage was considered a serious sin, though perhaps less so if performed before ensoulment" (https://embryo.asu.edu/pages/st-augustine-354-430). In a sermon on Genesis 24:1-4, Martin Luther (1483-1546) said, "How great, therefore, the wickedness of human nature is! How many girls there are who prevent conception and kill and expel tender fetuses, although procreation is the work of God" (Luther, *Lectures on Genesis*. Concordia Publishing House, 1986, p. 304; see https://carm.org/abortion-and-the-protestant-reformers).

John Calvin (1509-1564) wrote, "The fetus, though enclosed in the womb of its mother, is already a human being, and it is an almost monstrous crime to rob it of the life which it has not yet begun to enjoy. If it seems more horrible to kill a man in his own house than in a field because a man's house is his place of most secure refuge, it ought surely to be deemed more atrocious to destroy a fetus in the womb before it has come to light" (Calvin, *Harmony of the Law*, Volume 3, Commentary on Exodus 21:22; https://carm.org/abortion-and-the-protestant-reformers).

The Roman Catholic Church has stood against abortion for centuries. The Vatican website claims, "Since the first century, the Church has affirmed the moral evil of every procured abortion. This teaching has not changed and remains unchangeable. Direct abortion, that is to say, abortion willed either as an end or a means, is gravely contrary to the moral law" (see article at https://www.vatican.va/archive/ENG0015/__P7Z.HTM).

Historically, Protestant churches have taught that abortion is immoral, but when the mother's life is in danger, it is the lesser of two evils. Some Protestants would also include incest and rape as acceptable reasons for abortion.

Colonial America There is a difference of opinion about the belief and practice of abortion in the early United States. One view is, "Prior to the 1840s, abortion was widespread and not illegal. Under the Puritans, abortion was allowed until the fetus was 'quick' or until the woman could feel it move even up to the fourth or fifth month, as it was the woman's choice. For more than two centuries after the Pilgrims landed, abortion was largely permitted" (see the article at https://azcapitoltimes.com/news/2019/09/16/abortion-legal-under-puritans-more-than-200-years-what-changed/). Given their Calvinistic theology, it is hard to imagine that the Puritans allowed abortion until quickening. Is that true?

It is not exactly accurate to say that abortion was "not illegal" during the colonial period. It would be more accurate to say, "During the colonial period, the legality of abortion varied from colony to colony and reflected the attitude of the European country which controlled the specific colony. In the British colonies, abortions were legal if they were performed prior to quickening. In the French colonies, abortions were frequently performed despite the fact that they were considered to be illegal. In the Spanish and Portuguese colonies, abortion was illegal" (see the article at https://pubmed.ncbi.nlm.nih.gov/10297561/).

The British colonies might not have had a law against abortion, but the New England colonies were founded by Puritans who were opposed to abortion. "During the Elizabethan era, there was a considerable body of knowledge concerning birth control techniques, including coitus interruptus, penis ointments, pessaries, purgatives, genital baths, and bloodletting. Works were available describing the symptoms and causes of abortion and reporting some abortifacients. The Puritans were aware of birth control techniques but were opposed to them for several reasons: 1) it would go against the biblical injunction to be fruitful and multiply; 2) birth control frustrated the creation of what was in the image of God; 3) fecundity was a blessing and should not be thwarted; 4) the society of the elect should be increased; and 5) through childbirth a woman could atone for Eve's original sin. Although some Puritans recognized that marriage was for comfort and solace as well as for the bearing of progeny, birth control was frowned upon, and the Puritan clergy practiced what they preached. In a random sample of Puritan clergy, there was an average of 6.8 children born per family, which was higher than the average to be found among the English nobility of the same period" (https://pubmed.ncbi.nlm.nih.gov/11619425/).

Whether or not abortion was widespread has also been questioned. Joseph W. Dellapenna (who holds Law degrees from several Universities) was a professor at Villanova University from 1976 to 2016. In the 1300-page tome *Dispelling the Myths of Abortion History* (2006), Dellapenna covered the history of abortion and abortion law in England and American society. He wrote, "Anglo-American law always treated abortion as a serious crime, generally including early in pregnancy. Prosecutions and executions go back 800 years in England, establishing a law that carried over to colonial America. The reasons offered for these prosecutions and penalties consistently focused on protecting the life of the unborn child. This unbroken tradition refutes the claims that unborn children have not been treated as persons in our law or as persons under the Constitution of the United States" (https://cap-press.com/books/isbn/9780890895092/Dispelling-the-Myths-of-Abortion-History).

Keown says, "Professor Dellapenna's scholarly volume is now the leading work on the history of abortion in the United States. He shows that the criminal law prohibited abortion from colonial times and did so primarily to protect the unborn. Although he is himself pro-choice, his book gravely undermines the prevailing pro-choice version of abortion history, and the reasoning of the Supreme Court in ROE v WADE, that a constitutional right to abortion is consistent with the nation's history and traditions" (*John Keown, Professor at Georgetown University* (https://cap-press.com/books/isbn/9780890895092/Dispelling-the-Myths-of-Abortion-History).

Another author has questioned the prevailing view. Marvin Olasky (Ph.D. University of Michigan) was a professor at the University of Texas (1983-2007), provost of The King's College (2007-2011, and Patrick Henry College's distinguished chair in journalism and public policy (2011-2019). In *Abortion Rites: A Social History of Abortion in America* (1992), Olasky traces abortion from Colonial times to 1930. Here are excerpts from that book.

Olasky says, "Solid statistics concerning early abortion and even unwed pregnancy are unavailable, but I have looked at enough pre-1800 records of infanticide and abortion to see a pattern emerging.... The records suggest that, overall, infanticide was probably the most frequent way of killing unwanted, illegitimate children.... Physical and social reasons made abortion the less preferred mode of infant murder. Surgical abortion was virtually a guaranteed double-killer due to poor knowledge of anatomy and the great risk of infection. Abortifacients were known and used in early America, however.

"Historians have differed on how often abortifacients were used in colonial days and how 'effectual' they were; the anecdotal evidence, which is all we have in this and many other abortion-related issues, is mixed.... Since ingesting savin or other abortifacients was like playing Russian roulette with three bullets in the chambers, it is unlikely that colonial women would use the substances voluntarily unless they felt they had no other choice. How often they would feel such hopelessness brings us to consideration the social climate concerning premarital sexual relations and consequent out-of-wedlock conceptions. The pressure was largely religious, familial, and churchly."

"Behind the physical and social checks on abortion loomed the theological and the scientific.... At a time when sermons were the major means of communication and public affairs analysis, New England was filled with Presbyterian and Congregationalist churches founded on the doctrines of John Calvin, who wrote that an unborn child, 'though enclosed in the womb of its mother, is already a human being' and should not be 'rob[bed] of the life which it has not yet begun to enjoy.' A host of other Calvinists criticized 'those who, by the same forbidden lust or violent abortions of offspring, destroy it before it was born. ...' The Anglican Church, dominant in other parts of the country, and Lutheran churches as well, strongly opposed abortion.

"English books available in the American colonies also included strong injunctions against abortion.... Nicholas Culpeper, writing about drugs that could be used in cases of menstrual obstruction, told midwives, 'give not any of those to any that is with child, lest you turn Murtherers, wilful Murther seldom goes unpunished in this World, never in that to come.' Benjamin Wadsworth, later to be president of Harvard College, declared in 1712 that 'If any purposely endeavor [sic] to destroy the Fruit of their Womb (whether they actually do it or not) they're guilty of Murder in God's account.'

"During the seventeenth and eighteenth centuries, many scientists essentially believed human life to begin not *after* quickening but *before* quickening. Anton von Leeuwenhoek's discovery of microscopic 'animalcules' in 1674 gave a boost to old theories that humans were actually 'preformed' and existed as little people within the sperm.... In any event, with physical, social, theological, and "scientific" reasons all making abortion unacceptable, only those in extreme duress or with contempt for existing standards would resort to it. Since there were no pregnancy tests and early signs of possible pregnancy could be misleading, few women were likely to attempt early abortions, even if they wished to play abortifacient roulette.

"How frequent was abortion? We know of the occasional incidents, but we have no reliable statistics. It is worth noting that colonial court records are filled with reports of flogging, fornication, and fraud; colonies and municipalities adopted statutes directed at everyday crimes, but they evidently had far less need to act on abortion. However, ... New York City, on July 27, 1716, enacted an ordinance that forbade midwives to aid in or recommend abortion and thus severely limited access to abortion services. All midwives were required to swear that they would 'not Give any Counsel or Administer any Herb Medicine or Potion, or any other thing to any Woman being with Child whereby She Should Destroy or Miscarry of that she goeth with all before her time.'

"At no time was abortion considered legitimate and legal, but the practice did occur when some women fell through the cracks, taking their unborn children with them." (https://world.wng.org/2015/01did_colonial_america_have_abortions_yes_but).

After 1776 "From 1776 until the mid-1800s, abortion was viewed as socially unacceptable; however, abortions were not illegal in most states. During the 1860s, a number of states passed anti-abortion laws. Most of these laws were ambiguous and difficult to enforce. After the 1860s, stronger anti-abortion laws was passed, and these laws were more vigorously enforced" (https://pubmed.ncbi.nlm.nih.gov/10297561/).

"In the mid-to late-1800s, an increasing number of states passed anti-abortion laws sparked by both moral and safety concerns. Primarily motivated by fears about high risks for injury or death, medical practitioners in particular, led the charge for anti-abortion laws during this era. By 1860, the American Medical Association sought to end legal abortion. The Comstock Law of 1873 criminalized attaining, producing, or publishing information about contraception, sexually transmitted infections and diseases, and how to procure an abortion" (https://news.osu.edu/a-concise-history-of-the-us-abortion-debate/).

Conclusion In many places in colonial America, abortion was illegal, and even where there were no laws against it, it was socially unacceptable; later, it became illegal.

Summary: From the beginning, Christian values influenced the society of the U.S., meaning, as a rule, the Bible was respected, God, at least as Creator, was acknowledged, and people believed in moral responsibility. As a result, the traditional family was the norm, students in school were exposed to Christianity, capitalism was the economic system, the rule of law was the rule, and the sanctity of life, at least in the area of abortion, was accepted.

Fred Chay, Professor of Theology and Dean of the Doctoral Studies program at Grace School of Theology, said, "Christian Theists and Deists founded our unique and exceptional country. Christianity and its Judeo-Christian value system influenced everything from economics to education and has radically changed the world both for the temporal and eternal good of millions of people" ("Friday with Fred" blog post, 1/24/2020).

The Bible, in general, and the Ten Commandments, in particular, contain the values that permeated society at the founding of the U.S. God is to be acknowledged (Commandments 1-4). Moral responsibility is to be practiced (Commandments 6-9). The traditional family is to teach children honor and obedience (Commandment 5; see Deuteronomy 6:4-9). People have the right to own property (Commandment 8; you shall not steal). Life is sacred (Commandment 6; you shall not murder). Those values made America great. The Ten Commandments teach us that there will be no objective moral responsibility if there is no recognition of God and no functional families. So, to kill the United States of America, you need to discredit the Bible and depart from the Ten Commandments.

Chapter 3

DEATH IN THE U.S. SOCIETY

Obviously, Christian values do not influence the society of the U.S. today as they did for the first hundred years of its existence. What happened? Like slow-growing cancer, over a long process, a disease of ideas began to infect the U.S. The U.S. was founded in the 18th century. It began to unravel spiritually and morally in the 19th century as *concepts* were proposed that discredited the Bible, dethroned God, discounted moral responsibility, etc. These different *ideas* slowly changed society. What were those ideas? This chapter will answer that question. It is about thinkers whose ideas changed the way people in America think.

Discrediting The Bible

Classic theological liberalism arose out of German rationalism. In the middle of the 19th century, German theologians rejected the supernatural and replaced revelation with reason.

Immanuel Kant Immanuel Kant (1724-1804) provided the *philosophical* framework for biblical criticism and theological liberalism (Cairns, p. 410). He rejected the rational arguments for the existence of God (Eerdmans', p. 543). According to Kant, the Bible is a man-made book that was to be subjected to historical criticism (called "higher criticism") like any other book.

There was no place for Christ as the God-man.

Frederick Schleiermacher Frederick D. E. Schleiermacher (1768-1834) is the "father of liberalism" (González, II, p. 287). He was reared in the home of a Reformed pastor, who had Moravian tendencies (González, II, p. 285) and was trained in Moravian schools (Pietism), where he learned the subjective side of Christianity (Cairns, p. 410). He studied under Kant and accepted Kant's criticism of the proofs for the existence of God (Eerdmans' p. 543). When the rationalism of his time made it difficult for him to continue holding several of the traditional doctrines of Christianity, he made feelings or emotions the basis of spiritual experience. In *Discourses on Religion* (1799), Schleiermacher defined religion as an intuition or feeling for the universe, often described as an awareness of God. In *The Christian Faith* (*ca.* 1821), he presented religion not as a set of beliefs and obligations but as the result of man's feelings of absolute dependence (Cairns, pp. 410-411). By "feeling," he did not mean a passive emotion or sudden experience but rather a profound awareness of the existence of One on which all existence depends. The doctrine of creation is important because it affirms that all existence depends on God, but that does not mean that the Genesis account of creation is historically accurate. Schleiermacher himself did not think it was (González, II p. 286). Schleiermacher was also a pioneer of biblical criticism (Eerdmans', p. 541).

Julius Wellhausen According to the Bible, Moses wrote the first five books of the Bible. Wellhausen (1844-1918), an Old Testament professor in Germany, challenged that. In 1878, he wrote the *Prolegomena to the History of Israel*, which is the classic expression of what is known as the Documentary Hypothesis. The Documentary Hypothesis, also known as the JEDP theory, says that the material in the Pentateuch originated with four different authors, not just one.

About 850 BC, an unknown author in the Southern Kingdom (J) wrote the narrative sections that call God "Jehovah." An unknown author in the Northern Kingdom about 750 BC (E) wrote the narrative portions and employed "Elohim," the Hebrew word for God. About 650 BC, an unknown editor, called a redactor, combined J and E into a single document. Then, another unknown author called the Deuteronomist (D) wrote during the reforms of Josiah about 621 BC to compel the people in the Southern Kingdom to abandon their local "high places" and bring their sacrifices to the Temple in Jerusalem. Finally, the priestly portions (P) were composed from about 570 BC to the Exile. In other words, the Pentateuch was edited and revised from these documents, perhaps as late as 200 BC.

If the Documentary Hypothesis is correct, Moses did not write the Pentateuch about 1400 BC. In short, the Old Testament is not historically correct. By the way, the Documentary Hypothesis is bogus. There is no documentary evidence. No J, E, D, or P documents have been discovered. They only exist in the minds of critics.

"Before Wellhausen came on the scene, the Bible was generally accepted as the revealed, true, and inerrant Word of God.... In the Bible, we had a book we could trust" (Breese, p. 91). Breese explains that until the middle of the 19th century, if people called themselves "religious," it meant that they were orthodox Protestant, Orthodox Catholic, or Orthodox Jew. "The Bible was the authoritative book, the government was to be respected, the order in society was to be kept—that's the way it was" (Breese, p. 90). Wellhausen and other German theologians turned that around. They placed reason above revelation and concluded that the Bible could not be seriously trusted. The Bible was not the Word of God; it was a collection of human documents.

Charles A. Briggs Charles A. Briggs (1841-1913) studied in Germany, where he accepted the critical view of Scripture. In 1874, he became a professor at Union Theological Seminary in New York City. In 1889, he wrote *Whither? A Theological Question for the Times*, in which he sharply criticized the inerrancy of Scripture. As the head of the new Department of Biblical Theology, Briggs delivered an inaugural address on January 20, 1891. In it, he stated there were four barriers keeping people from the Bible: superstition, verbal inspiration, inerrancy, and belief that the authenticity of the Bible is founded upon the idea that holy men of old wrote holy writ. He said Moses and David were no more inspired than Confucius. Moses did not write the Pentateuch. David only wrote a few of the Psalms. Isaiah did not write all of the books that bear his name. On another occasion, Briggs said Daniel did not write the book of Daniel.

Theological Liberalism Among other things, theological liberalism denies the inerrancy of Scripture. It is impossible to determine an exact date for the beginning of theological liberalism in America, but it has been suggested that it may be dated by the inaugural address given by Briggs in 1891. Cooper claims it was the first public affirmation of liberalism in a seminary in the U.S. (Cooper, p. 55). Lindsell points out that theological liberalism was in the seminary before Briggs, but Briggs was the catalyst that brought the trend in the seminary to the light of day (Lindsell, p. 191).

To gain prestigious degrees, American professors went to Germany for theological education (for example, Briggs). Thus, theological liberalism was "transmitted to America by American students of theology who studied German philosophy and biblical criticism in German and Scottish universities" (Cairns, p. 444). They brought back theological liberalism to American seminaries. It did not take long before the pastors trained under such professors were preaching theological liberalism in their churches. "By 1900, the ideas of the universal fatherhood of God and the brotherhood of man had spread from the seminaries to the laity" (Cairns, p. 444).

The Result The net result of all of this is that the Bible has been discredited. "As the Bible became more and more a human book, it became more and more irrelevant" (Breese, p. 206).

In 2013, research by the Barna Group reported that 77% of the people in the U.S. believed "the values and morals of America are declining." And "nearly six out of ten adults (56%) believe the Bible has too little influence in American society" (https://www.barna.com/research/what-do-americans-really-think-about-the-bible/).

In 2017, according to the Gallup Poll, "Fewer than one in four Americans (24%) now believe the Bible is 'the actual word of God, and is to be taken literally, word for word,' similar to the 26% who view it as 'a book of fables, legends, history and moral precepts recorded by man.' This is the first time in Gallup's four-decade trend that biblical literalism has not surpassed biblical skepticism. Meanwhile, about half of Americans—a proportion largely unchanged over the years—fall in the middle, saying the Bible is the inspired word of God but that not all of it should be taken literally" (https://news.gallup.com/poll/210704/record-few-americans-believe-bible-literal-word-god.aspx, accessed August 22, 2019).

Also. in 2017, the Pew Research Center found that only 45% of the people in the U.S. could name all four Gospels (https://www.pewresearch.org/fact-tank/2017/04/14/5-facts-on-how-americans-view-the-bible-and-other-religious-texts/ft_17-04-12_scripture_frequency_by_trad/).

In a short video for Prager University, John Eastman, Professor of Law at Chapman University and a Senior Fellow at the Claremont

Institute, pointed out that "They [The Founding Fathers] saw religion—specifically religions based on the Bible—as indispensable to the moral foundation of the nation they were creating.... [Then], in the case of *Everson v. Board of Education*, the Supreme Court ruled in a 5-4 decision that under the First Amendment, neither a state nor the Federal Government could pass laws that aid one religion, aid all religions, or prefer one religion over another.... For Jefferson and the other Founders, religion was central to the entire American project. The Declaration of Independence and the Constitution are just two of countless examples where the government acknowledges its debt to God.... Following Everson, the nation's moral infrastructure began to crack—at first slowly and then more rapidly.... Are we a better society for it? It's hard to argue that we are. Almost every cultural and ethical indicator—marriage rates, birth rates, the number of Americans giving to charity—has declined since God and religion have faded from American life. Meanwhile, children without fathers in their lives, behavioral problems in schools, and crime have gone up dramatically. And all because of one vote, in one court case, based on one sentence in one letter" (Eastman; https://www.prageru.com/video/what-does-separation-of-church-and-state-mean/).

In 2019, my brother Dr. John Cocoris, a therapist in Dallas, Texas, in the process of counseling a schoolteacher, used the story of Adam and Eve to make a point. During the conversation, he discovered she did not know the story of Adam and Eve was in the Bible! Imagine a teacher not knowing one of the most elementary elements of the best-selling book of all time. The Bible, which started as the basis of education in the U.S., is now banned in schools.

Today, in the U.S., the Bible is dead in schools and most of American society.

Death in the U.S. Society

Dethroning God

The Civil War In many ways, the Civil War was a major turning point in American history. Peter H. Irons, a political science professor at the University of California, San Diego, said, "The Civil War changed American society in profound and lasting ways" (Irons, Lecture 8). It not only freed the slaves, but it also made the national government prominent over the states. Furthermore, it had an impact on religion. As Guelzo points out, "Religious confidence was especially traumatized. The randomness of death wrecked peacetime faith in God. Never again would evangelical Christianity so dominate public life" (Guelzo, p. 56). In addition, corporations became a major factor in American life. Men who made fortunes through corporations founded universities. Ezra Cornell, the founder of Western Union, was co-founder of Cornell University. J. D. Rockefeller, the founder of the Standard Oil company, founded the University of Chicago and Leland Stanford, who made his fortune building the transcontinental railroad, founded Stanford University in honor of his only son, who died of typhoid fever. "Between 1848 and 1870, 35 colleges established scientific departments" (Guelzo, p. 58). In the meantime, there was a growing selfish individualism. Henry Adams, the grandson of John Quincy Adams and the great-grandson of John Adams, spoke about the "cesspool of selfishness" (Guelzo, Lecture 19). There was also a growing indifference to religion. Religion became marginalized (Guelzo, p. 58).

Darwinism Charles Darwin (1809-1882) studied medicine at Edinburgh, but when he could not stomach surgery without anesthetics, he studied for the ministry at Cambridge. In his autobiography, he wrote, "I did not then in the least doubt the strict and literal truth of every word in the Bible, I soon persuaded myself that our creed [of the Church of England] must be fully accepted" (Darwin, cited by Breese, pp. 24-25).

While still in college, he became interested in natural history. As a result of his interest in natural history, Darwin took a five-year cruise (1826-1830) to survey the shores of Chile, Peru, and some of the islands in the Pacific. On that trip, he collected plants, insects, etc. Later, he raised pigeons and carefully observed their development. He also paid attention to various flowers in his garden, collecting "data" from these observations. Based on data collected on his trip and five years of work, Darwin developed a theory to account for how various species came to be differentiated. In 1859, Darwin wrote *Origin of the Species*.

As Darwin himself explained, more individuals of a species are born than can survive, and consequently, there is a struggle for existence. The individuals within the species that developed a slight variation have a better chance of surviving and are thus naturally selected. The selected ones reproduce in their modified form. Later, Herbert Spencer coined the phrase "survival of the fittest."

Darwin knew his "data" did not conclusively prove his theory. He said, "I am well aware that scarcely a single point is discussed in this volume in which facts cannot be advanced, often apparently leading to conclusions directly opposite to those at which I have arrived" (Darwin, cited by Breese, p. 27). In addition, as Breese pointed out, "When Charles Darwin wrote *Origin of the Species*, he told us nothing about origins. Rather, he spoke only of processes through which he believed biological life replicated itself upward, successive generations reproducing from the simple to the complex. But this theory was arbitrarily distilled from his observation of present life forms and residues. It was not based on empirical observation, for no observer but God was present to observe the beginning of things.

The scientist who says, 'This is the way it all began,' is not speaking as a scientist, but rather as a speculator on a par with all others who speculate about beginnings" (Breese, p. 40).

Nevertheless, within a few decades, Darwin's *theory* was accepted by the academic community as the explanation of the origin of human beings. "The early 1900s was the first era in which Darwin and his ideas had come to full flower. By that time, evolution was well on its way to capturing the world of academia and the thought processes of the average man" (Breese, p. 153). One author said that Darwin's theory was "probably the most revolutionary change that is ever occurred in man's view of himself.... It demands that we regard ourselves as inseparably a part of nature and accept the fact that our descent was from more primitive creatures, and, ultimately, from a common origin of all life on earth" (William Sullivan in the 1972 introduction to Darwin's *The Voyage of the Beagle*, p. vii, cited by Breese, p. 24). Guelzo wrote, "Whereas Puritans ... had once been able to tell Americans to improve themselves for the glory of God, Social Darwinism allowed them to pursue self-improvement for the good of the species" (Guelzo, p. 60).

Darwinism not only changed our view of ourselves, it dethroned God as the Creator. In 2006, the evolutionary botanist Richard Dawkins wrote *The God Delusion*. He maintained that post-Darwin scientific advances had rendered any belief in God irrational and unnecessary (Horowitz, p. 7). Dawkins wrote, "The God of the Old Testament is arguably the most unpleasant character in all fiction: jealous and proud of it; a petty, unjust, unforgiving control-freak; a vindictive, bloodthirsty ethnic cleanser; a misogynistic, homophobic, racist, infanticidal, genocidal, filicidal, pestilential, megalomaniacal, sadomasochistic, capriciously, malevolent bully" (Dawkins, cited by Horowitz, p. 8). As Horowitz goes on to explain if God is God,

His megalomanil (delusions of grandeur) is not a delusion and "control freak" is implicit in His job description (Horowitz, p.9). At any rate, the point is "evolution's dethronement of God" (Guelzo, p. 68).

The Scopes Trial In 1925, John Scopes, a substitute high school biology teacher, was accused of violating a Tennessee law that made it unlawful to teach human evolution in any state-funded school. This was deliberately planned to challenge the teaching of evolution. Scopes was not even sure he had ever taught evolution; he purposefully incriminated himself. Scopes lost the trial, but his conviction was overturned on a technicality. The trial received intense national publicity. It was seen as a trial on whether or not modern science should be taught in schools. As a result of the trial, Bible-believing Christians were thought of as uneducated and ignorant. The debate over evolution has been said to have far-reaching implications in moving the U.S. toward a secular society.

The Result In 1963, a Supreme Court ruling stated, "only last year [1962] an official survey of the country indicated that ... less than 3% profess no religion whatsoever (*Abington Township v. Schempp*, at 203, 213, cited by Barton, p. 166). According to the third American Family Survey (2019), 33% of the people in the United States identified as "nones" ("atheists," "agnostics," "nothing in particular"), up from 30% in 2015.

In an article based on the largest study ever conducted on changes in Americans' religious involvement, Jean M. Twenge wrote that as compared to the 1980s, "Twice as many high school seniors, and three times as many college students, described their religion as 'none' in the 2010s.... 75% more 12th graders said that religion was 'not important at all' in their lives.... things are changing, fast.... Millennials are the least religious generation in the last six decades.

If we assume that Americans in the 1950s and earlier were just as religious as those in the 1970s, Millennials are the least religious generation in American history.... More adolescents now say that their parents don't affiliate with a religion, suggesting they were raised without religion at all" (Jean M. Twenge, *Psychology Today*, "The Real Reason Religion is Declining In America," https://www.psychologytoday.com/us/blog/our-changing-culture/201505/the-real-reason-religion-is-declining-in-america).

In the thinking of many Americans today, God has not only been dethroned, He is no longer needed. Chuck Colson (1931-2012), founder of Prison Fellowship and author of over thirty books, told of a thirteen-year-old student who answered the question on a weekly quiz, "Where did the earth come from?" by saying "God created it" and was marked off twenty points. He was supposed to say "the Big Bang" (Charles Colson, "Quoting the Bible Isn't Enough." *Christianity Today*, August 11, 1997). A big bang has replaced the Creator.

In 1983, Aleksandr Solzhenitsyn, the famous Russian political prisoner, author, and historian, delivered a speech in London in which he said, "If I were called upon to identify briefly the principal trait of the *entire* twentieth century, here too, I would be unable to find anything more precise and pithy than to repeat once again: "*Men have forgotten God*" (Solzhenitsyn, italics his, http://orthochristian.com/47643.html).

Today, in the U.S. society at large, God is dethroned, not needed, and forgotten. To many Americans, He is as good as dead. The cover story for the April 8, 1966 edition of *Time* magazine was "Is God Dead?"

Discounting Moral Responsibility

Freud Sigmund Freud (1856-1939) earned his medical degree from the University of Vienna. Of the more than 20 books Freud wrote, several are particularly significant. In 1895, Freud and German physician Josef Breuer published *Studies in Hysteria*. At this point, the theory was that unconscious emotions resulted in physical symptoms called Hysteria. In 1899, Freud Wrote *The Interpretation of Dreams*. In 1923, He wrote *Ego and the Id* and in 1939, *Moses and Monotheism*.

Freud's analysis of people is that they consist of an id (the pleasure principle, the drive to personal gratification of sex and aggression), the superego (their moral code), and the ego (the executive that governs the person). The essence of Freud's elaborate theory is that neurosis begins with the id (the drives of sex and aggression). Because of neurotic anxiety (the fear that a drive will get out of control and cause punishment), the ego uses defense mechanisms to cope with the anxiety and not be overwhelmed. Anxiety operates at an unconscious level. As this unconscious anxiety attempts to intrude into consciousness, the person begins to panic, and symptoms appear.

To say the same thing another way, unconscious, unresolved conflicts between the id (sex and aggression drives) and the ego during the first six years of life overwhelm the ego, creating anxiety and neurotic symptoms. The basic conflict centers on the unconscious, incestuous desire for the parent of the opposite sex. There is also the unconscious wish to "do away with" the competition, the parent of the same sex. Since these feelings are threatening, they are repressed.

Freudianism teaches that *unconscious, unresolved conflicts in early childhood determine all human behavior*. Past events undoubtedly influence people, but Freud's determinism discounts personal responsibility. Some would go so far as to say Freud's view "has encouraged irresponsible people to persist in and expand their irresponsibility" (Adams, p. 17). To say that Freud's view "encouraged" irresponsibility might not be precisely accurate, but the kind of determinism Freud helped popularize discounts personal responsibility.

Kierkegaard Soren Kierkegaard (1813-1855) was a Lutheran Danish philosopher, theologian, and religious author. "He gave the world what philosophers call *existentialism*. He gave the church what theologians call *neo-orthodoxy*" (Breese, p. 210, italics his). Kaufmann said, "The refusal to belong to any school of thought, the repudiation of the adequacy of any body of beliefs of whatever, and especially of systems, and a marked dissatisfaction with traditional philosophy as superficial, academic, and remote from life—that is the heart of existentialism" (Kaufmann, cited by Breese, p. 216). For him, only the individual has significance. He also renounced thinking.

For the existentialist, "this moment" is the ultimate thing. Atheistic existentialists deny any consistent morality. For them, "the only right is what is right for you, and the only wrong is that which produces pain or inconvenience for you. There is no law, principle, or proper course of action of any kind, so go with the vibes! Whatever is your thing, do it" (Breese, p. 217). Existentialism "is not simply another point of view, but rather it is a denial of all points of view. Far from redefining truth, existentialism announces that there is no truth. There is neither final proof nor immediate truth. There is only this one moment, without cause and without consequences" (Breese, p. 218).

Although Kierkegaard lived in the 19th century, it was not until after World War II that he became influential in America. According to Breese, who wrote in 1990, existentialism "has become the most pervasive philosophy of our time. There is virtually no philosophy department in any major university in Western civilization that is not built on an existentialist base.... Existentialism produced the raging, resentful youth society of the 1960s" (Breese, p. 217).

The 1960s Revolution The 1960s was a decade of protest and revolution that changed American society. The movements of the era included the civil rights movement, the anti-Vietnam War movement, the women's movement, the gay rights movement, and the environmental movement. It was a time of social upheaval with massive rallies and riots. Within the span of five years, President John F. Kennedy, Martin Luther King Jr., and Robert Kennedy were assassinated. The decade of the 1960s has been called one of the most disruptive eras in American history. Young people formed a counterculture that rebelled against long-standing customs, personal behavior, and music, which played an important role in defining the character and spirit of the time. Timothy Leary promoted experiments with hallucinogenic drugs. His slogan was, "Turn on, tune in, drop out." Part of this revolution was the sexual revolution. Politically, Lyndon Baines Johnson (1908–1973), the 36th President of the U.S. from 1963 to 1969, made big government (Franklin Delano Roosevelt's New Deal) bigger (the Great Society). "Since the 1960s, students have been told that everything is relative, the judgment is verboten, and if it feels good, do it, while decency and morality are cast as deviant concepts used by the oppressor" (Bruce, p. 162).

The Result As a result of such things as determinism, existentialism, and the social/sexual revelation of the 1960s, moral absolutes, as expressed in the Ten Commandments, have been replaced by moral relativism. In the Christian value system, God is the source of moral values and, therefore, what is moral and immoral transcends personal or societal opinion. Without God, each individual or society makes his/her own moral standards. There is no longer an objective standard of right and wrong; now, right and wrong for a matter of personal opinion. The new rule is no rules.

For example, in 2003, Tammy Bruce, a conservative non-Christian lesbian, wrote a book entitled *The Death of Right and Wrong*. She describes a time in her life when "My entire focus was on me—what *I* wanted, what *I* was going to get, how much money *I* was going to make. There were no moral standards in my life. It was a world of self-indulgent narcissism.... If it felt good, I did it. It was this self-absorption that facilitated the view of myself as a Victim.... After all, I wasn't responsible for the things that happened in my life (especially the bad things). Someone else had to be" (Bruce, p. 5, italics hers). She goes on to say she was "morally bankrupt" because her "moral relativism" kept her from looking at any part of her life with "any kind of a value-based perspective" (Bruce, p. 6) and that a "moral vacuum ... corrupts our culture and threatens our very liberty" (Bruce, p. 7). She quotes Oriana Fallaci, who said, "Freedom cannot exist without discipline, self-discipline" (Bruce, p. 9). She adds, welcome to the culture where right and wrong have taken such a beating, they are no longer recognizable (Bruce, p. 11).

Dr. Camille Paglia is a humanities and media studies professor at the University of the Arts in Philadelphia. She is an atheist who describes herself as transgender. In an interview that appeared in the *Wall Street Journal*, she complained that the current generation has been raised in a climate where personal responsibility isn't spoken of ("A Feminist Capitalist Professor Under Fire" by Tunku Varadarajan.

The Wall Street Journal, Aug. 30, 2019).

The moral responsibility issue is not just a Christian issue. A non-Christian, even an atheist, recognizes that moral responsibility is no longer the norm in America.

Today, in the U.S. society at large, objective moral responsibility is dead.

Decline of the Traditional Family

Family Living In 2003, I wrote an article describing the decline in family living. In it, I said, "God intended for parents and children to live together *as a family* (Deut. 6:7-9). When America was first founded and immigrants, armed with a Judeo-Christian heritage, poured onto American soil, the social structure was such that living as a family was the norm…. Children *spent time with their parents*. Then, *family living* began to decline. 1) The Industrial Revelation made America more urban. Urban fathers worked outside the home. 2) The automobile made the family more mobile, which took them outside the home more, but the family still lived in neighborhoods. In the neighborhood, there was a sense of community in that people knew their neighbors and their neighbors knew them. 3) When World War II came, the men left home to go to war and the women left home to go to the factories. When the war ended, the men came home and the women didn't. The extra income was nice for extra things and there were more things to buy. Nevertheless, although the neighbors were not as close, there was still the neighborhood. Neighborhoods had sidewalks! Homes built before 1974 have sidewalks. Sidewalks gave people another opportunity to meet and greet their neighbors. Many newer communities lack sidewalks, so residents tend to drive

("Where you live affects your life," *Parade Magazine*, August 3, 2003, p. 9). 4) Before World War II, the radio began to occupy the evenings of many. In the 1950s, TV replaced the radio as the activity of choice in the evening. 5) In the meantime, the car, the sexual revelation, birth control, and abortion took teens more and more out of the house and away from the influence and ideals of the home. 6) As the population grew and cities expanded, Americans became more and more suburban. In suburbia, there were fewer and fewer sidewalks and more and more driveways. There was less and less sense of family and community. 7) By the end of the twentieth century, the very nature of the family was being redefined. Many children had been reared by one parent. In 1960, every state in the U.S. had a law against homosexuality. Now, homosexuals want to be legally married! As a result of these changes, the definition of "family" has changed. Many are confused as to what a family is supposed to be…. Family living is no longer the norm." Since I wrote that article, same-sex marriage is now legal.

Divorce In 2018, *Time* magazine put the divorce rate at 39%. It said, "Experts now put your chances of uncoupling at about 39% in the U.S." (https://time.com/5434949/divorce-rate-children-marriage-benefits/).

Cohabitation "The US Senate Joint Economic Committee—Republicans" states, "As marriage has declined, couples have become more likely to cohabit as unmarried couples. In the 1960s, less than one percent of couples lived together before marriage—a figure that rose to 5 percent by 1990 and stood at 12-13 percent as of 2019…. Furthermore, marriage is much more likely to be preceded by cohabitation today than in the past. Among women ages 19 to 44 who married between 1965 and 1974, just 11 percent had cohabited with their husbands before marriage, but that number jumped to 32 percent among those who married between 1975 and 1979 and continued to soar thereafter. For the past two decades, two-thirds of new marrieds have been preceded by cohabitation" (see "The Demise of the Happy Two-Parent Home," July 2020, p. 8. https//www. Jee.senate.gov/public/_cache/files/84d5b05b-la58-4b3f-8c8d-2f94cfe4bb59/3-20-the-demise-of-thehappy-two-parent-home.pdf).

In a 2018 article, *Time* magazine declared, "Cohabiting is becoming a norm in most Westernized countries" (https://time.com/5434949/divorce-rate-children-marriage-benefits/). In 2019, Pew Research reported, "The number of U.S. adults cohabiting with a partner is rising. In addition to half of the US adults who were married, 7% cohabited in 2016. The number of Americans living with an unmarried partner reached about 18 million in 2016, up 29% since 2007. Roughly half of the cohabiters are younger than 35—but cohabitation is rising most quickly among Americans ages 50 and older (https//www.pewresearch.org/fact-tank/2019/02/13/8-facts-about-love-and-marriage/).

The Sexual Revolution Hugh Hefner (1926-2017) described his family as "conservative, Midwestern, Methodist." His mother wanted him to become a missionary. From 1944 to 1946, he served as a U.S. Army writer for a military newspaper. He graduated from the University of Illinois at Urbana–Champaign in 1949 with a Bachelor of Arts in Psychology and a double minor in Creative Writing and Art. In 1949, Hefner married Mildred Williams. Before the wedding, Mildred confessed that she had an affair while he was away in the army. He said it was "the most devastating moment of my life." Mildred allowed him to have sex with other women out of guilt for her own infidelity and in the hope that it would preserve their marriage. The two were divorced in 1959.

In 1953, Hefner launched *Playboy*. The first issue featured Marilyn Monroe from her 1949 nude calendar shoot. He published Charles Beaumont's science fiction story "The Crooked Man." It was the story of straight men being persecuted in a world of homosexuality. Hefner said, "If it was wrong to persecute heterosexuals in a homosexual society, then the reverse was wrong, too." Hugh Hefner advocated for "sexual liberation" and freedom of expression. He supported legalizing same-sex marriage and said if we do not have same-sex marriage, "we will turn back the sexual revolution and return to an earlier, puritanical time."

Suzanne Moore wrote in *The Guardian* that "part of Hefner's business acumen was to make the selling of female flesh respectable and hip and to make soft porn acceptable." In *The Independent*, Julie Bindel argued that Hefner "caused immeasurable damage by turning porn—and, therefore, the buying and selling of women's bodies—into a legitimate business." In the *Los Angeles Times*, Robin Abcarian wrote that Hefner "probably did more to mainstream the exploitation of women's bodies than any other figure in American history," adding that he "managed to convince many women that taking off their clothes for men's pleasure was not just empowering, but a worthy goal in itself."

In *Christianity Today*, Ed Stetzer lamented the consequences of Hefner's role as a "general" of the "sexual revolution." He wrote, "It's hard to fathom that anyone would have known what this would have turned into. Parents growing up today are fighting to keep their children pure. Spouses are fighting to keep their marriages intact. And many enslaved and trapped in the adult entertainment industry have been figuratively and literally stripped not only of their clothes but their very value as people made in the image of God. If this does not concern us, what will?" (*Ed Stetzer,* "Hugh Hefner, Mourning, and Legacies: Beyond the Pipe and the Robe," *Christianity Today*, September 28, 2017).

With the advent of Hugh Hefner, sex is not left for marriage; it is for pleasure without marriage. Thus, the devaluation of marriage. By the way, in 1992, Hefner told Alex Witchel of the New York Times, "I've spent so much of my life looking for love in all the wrong places" (Witchel, *New York Times*, November 22, 1992; see bibliography).

The Birth Control Pill Margaret Sanger (1879-1966) was the founder of the birth control movement in the U.S.; she is credited with originating the term 'birth control.' In 1914, she launched a monthly newspaper, the *Woman Rebel*, whose motto was, "No gods, No Masters!" (Horowitz, p. 77). In 1921, she founded the American Birth Control League, which later became the Planned Parenthood Federation of America. In 1951, Sanger met endocrinologist Gregory Pincus and persuaded him to work on a birth control pill. In 1957, the FDA approved his pill, but only for severe menstrual disorders, not as a contraceptive, but in 1960, the pill was approved as a contraceptive. It was only prescribed to married women until 1972.

Hugh Hefner popularized sex for fun instead of marriage; the birth control pill made sex safe, which encouraged sex outside of marriage.

Same-sex Marriage Homosexuality is as old as Sodom. It has been practiced behind closed doors throughout most of the history of the U.S., but that changed in the 1960s. Many homosexuals "came out" as a result of the Stonewall Riots. The Stonewall Inn was a gay hangout in Greenwich Village, New York. In June 1969, during a routine police raid, gay men, lesbians, and others fought back in the spirit of the civil rights movements of the time. The fear of homosexuals turned to anger. In the aftermath of the riots, many gay rights organizations formed, and a year later, the first Gay Pride March was held to mark the anniversary of the uprising. In 2015, in *Obergefell v. Hodges*, the Supreme Court struck down all state bans on same-sex marriage, legalizing it in all 50 states.

Individuality In the meantime, more and more emphasis has been put on the individual rather than the family. The issue of the right to privacy has played a part in this. In the landmark case, *Griswold v. Connecticut* (1965), the Supreme Court found that the law prohibiting birth control violated the constitutional right to marital privacy. *Griswold v. Connecticut* helped pave the way for *Roe v. Wade*, which said a "right of privacy" was "broad enough to encompass" a right to abortion. Notice the right to privacy moved from marital privacy to individual privacy. Also, due to women being given more freedom to pursue a career, there is less emphasis on marriage.

The Result Acceptance of premarital sex is at an all-time high. Marriage is on the decline. More young people are deciding not to marry even when they have children. In 1970, the percentage of births in the U.S. outside of marriage was 10%, but according to the United Nations Population Fund, in 2019, 40% of all births in the U.S. were outside of marriage. Also, as of 2019, approximately one out of every three children in the U.S. lives in a home without a father in residence (Michael Snyder; according to the CDC, in 2018, in the United States, 39.6% of all births were to unmarried women; https://www.cdc.gov/nchs/fastats/unmarried-childbearing.htm).

Today, in the U.S., the traditional family is in decline, becoming obsolete and virtually dead. In July 2020, a U.S. Senate committee concluded, "Unfortunately, family instability has increased to the point where it is the norm for many Americans today" (page 38; see the report (https/www.jec.senate.gov/public/_cache/file/84d5b05b-1a58-4b3f-8c8d-2f94cfe4bb59/3-20-the-demise-of-the-happy-two-parent-home.pdf).

Dumbing-down Education

Colleges Six of the eight Ivy League schools, Harvard, Yale, Princeton, Columbia, Dartmouth, and Brown, were founded by Protestants to prepare men for the ministry. At first, chapel was compulsory. Then it began to be discontinued. Harvard was first. Under the presidency of Unitarian Charles W. Eliot, Harvard abolished compulsory chapel in 1889. Princeton did not cancel compulsory chapel until 1962. "From the 1890s onward, college was where Americans were fitted for places in the American economy. The priorities in education shifted to the secular and the commercial" (Guelzo, p. 105).

John Dewey As was mentioned earlier (see "Christianity influenced Education" above), public education in the United States was gradually established until, by 1918, it was required in all states. The influence of the Bible in American education began to decline before John Dewey, but his ideas accelerated the process. John Dewey (1859-1952) was a professor at the University of Chicago (1894-1904) and at Columbia University (1904-1930). He wrote more than 700 articles in 140 journals and approximately 40 books. In 1899, he wrote his first major work on education, *The School and Society*. In 1916, he wrote *Democracy and Education*, his work on progressive education, and in 1934, he wrote *A Common Faith*, a humanistic study of religion. The overriding theme of Dewey's works was his profound belief in democracy, be it in politics, education, communication, or journalism. As Dewey himself stated in 1888, "Democracy and the one, ultimate, ethical ideal of humanity are to my mind synonymous." His biographer, Steven C. Rockefeller, traced Dewey's democratic convictions to his childhood attendance at the Congregational Church. It proclaimed the Social Gospel.

Dewey was critical of centering education on the curriculum and focusing almost solely on the subject matter to be taught. In his opinion, schools cultivated passive pupils by insisting on mastery of facts and disciplining bodies. In addition to helping students realize their full potential, education should be instrumental in creating social change and reform. He felt that the educational system must move "either backward to the intellectual and moral standards of prescientific age or forward to an ever-greater utilization of scientific method in the development of the possibilities of growing, expanding experience" (Dewey, cited by Breese, p. 162).

Dewey believed the educational system was a failure and needed revamping. As opposed to making students conversant with the "three R's," the educational system should make students adept at participation in the democratic process. He declared that "schools do have a role—an important one—in production of social change" (Dewey, cited by Breese, p. 163). Education and society need to move from the supernatural to the non-supernatural (Breese, p. 164). "Those who believe in religion ... must interest themselves in the transformation of those institutions which still bear the dogmatic and the feudal stamp till they are in accord with these [new] ideas" (Dewey, cited by Breese, p. 165).

As an atheist and a secular humanist in his later life, Dewey was one of the original 34 signatories of the first *Humanist Manifesto* (1933). In his 1934 book, *A Common Faith*, Dewey assured his readers that traditional religion was drifting into oblivion and would soon be a matter of interest only to history buffs. For him, as the automobile had supplanted the horse and buggy, so science would supplant religion. Astronomy had discredited "ascent into heaven." Geology had discredited creation in six days. Biology had dispatched the soul and the afterlife. Anthropology, history, and literary criticism have shown that revered religious figures and their deeds, if founded at all, were embellished to the point of fiction and psychology and that mystical and religious experiences had a natural explanation. As a result, Dewey expected that more and more educated people would abandon religion and its supernatural cast (God, salvation, grace, prayer, heaven, hell, the sacraments, clergy, revelation, the devil, etc.). He proposed a secular makeover of religion. Religious experience will no longer be a mystical encounter with a higher power but a courageous and persisting devotion to desirable social goals. Dewey wrote, "Any activity pursued in behalf of an ideal end against obstacles and in spite of threats of personal loss because of conviction of its general and enduring value is religious in quality." In addition, the term "God" will no longer apply to a deity but to "the unity of all ideal ends arousing us to desire and action."

Breese summarizes Dewey's ideas: 1) Final truth is illusory. The world is ever-changing. All reality is within the mind of the observer. Nothing is objectively true. 2) We must not think of truth but must concern ourselves with meaning. There is disagreement over what he meant by meaning. 3) Truth is resident in experience. Dewey railed against the lecture method as an inferior method of teaching. For him, truth does not consist in words, propositions, or assertions. People cannot claim to understand until they have experienced it. 4) Teaching fundamentally depends upon experience. Education is not students learning objective truths to think and act responsibly tomorrow; they can only discover what truth is for today. 5) The "idea of God" has meaning to those who believe. Religion, however, must be reformed to serve humanity. To Dewey, being dogmatic about anything was anathema (Breese, pp. 166-169). Guelzo says Dewey believed teaching was about preparing children for real life in a democracy. This education involved teaching useful trades and habits of tolerance and cooperative play and allowing the child to develop imagination (Guelzo, p. 72), adding that for Dewey, there are no absolutes and morals are nothing more than customs (Guelzo, Lecture 24).

Breese says that Dewey redefined almost everything from the nature of truth to the teacher's responsibilities (Breese, p. 155). "For him, nothing was constant, given, or finally true, but rather all things were pragmatic, adaptable, and subject to whatever reinterpretation seemed appropriate for the day and the hour" (Breese, p. 157).

John Dewey was a major voice of progressive education and liberalism. He was a major educational reformer of the 20th century. Historian Hilda Neatby wrote, "Dewey has been to our age what Aristotle was to the later Middle Ages, not a philosopher, but *the* philosopher." Historians consider Dewey the epitome of liberalism, and one (William R. Caspary) portrayed him as "dangerously radical." He identified himself as a democratic socialist. Historian Edward A. White suggested that Dewey's work led to the 20th-century rift between religion and science (White, *Science and Religion in American Thought*, 1952).

The Supreme Court As the number of public schools increased, they were controlled locally and reflected local culture. Bible reading and prayer were common. As public education became more centralized, the religious element became an issue (Guelzo, Lecture 36). Ultimately the religious issue ended up in the Supreme Court. The First Amendment to the Constitution says, "Congress shall make no law respecting an establishment of religion, or prohibiting the free exercise thereof, or abridging the freedom of speech, or of the press, or the right of the people peaceably to assemble, and to petition the Government for a redress of grievances." The first part about religion is known as the "establishment clause." Until the latter part of the 20th century, Congress, the Supreme Court, and the American people understood the establishment clause to mean: 1) *Congress* could not establish an official, national religion, and 2) *Congress* could not prohibit the free exercise of religion.

On October 7, 1801, the Baptist Association in Danbury, Connecticut, wrote President Thomas Jefferson expressing their concerns over the First Amendment. They felt that the "free exercise of religion" clause meant that the right was government-given (alienable, that is, able to take away) rather than God-given (inalienable, that is, unable to take away) and, therefore, someday the government might attempt to regulate religious expression (Barton, p. 50).

Jefferson's understanding of the First Amendment was that it prevented the *federal* government from establishing a *national Christian denomination*. In a letter dated September 23, 1800, Jefferson wrote to a fellow signer of the Declaration of Independence, Benjamin Rush, that every denomination, "especially the Episcopalians and Congregationalists," wanted to establish their form of Christianity throughout the U.S., but the Constitution secured the freedom of religion (Jefferson, *Memoirs*, vol. III, p. 441, cited by Barton, p. 51). On the eve of the Revolutionary, nine of the thirteen colonies had a "state" church. Only Rhode Island, Pennsylvania, New Jersey, and Delaware did not. Citizens in a colony with a state church had to pay a religious tax to support the state church. (Stevens, p. 10). Connecticut did not disestablish its state-sponsored church until 1818 and Massachusetts did not disestablish it until 1833. In other words, the Constitution prevented the *federal* government from establishing a *national* church but did not prohibit *states* from establishing a *state* church (Barton, pp. 30-31, 33). Jefferson understood that. In a letter to Samuel Miller (January 23, 1808), Jefferson declared that the "power to prescribe any religious exercise

... must rest with the States" (Jefferson, *Memoirs*, vol. IV, p. 104, cited by Barton, p. 54). "The Founder's sole intent was to prevent the federal establishment of a single denomination of Christianity" (Barton, p. 156).

So, in his reply to the Danbury Baptist Association (January 1, 1802), Jefferson wrote that the First Amendment built "a wall of separation between church and state" (Jefferson, *Writings*, vol. XVI, pp. 281-282, cited by Barton, p. 52). Jefferson's letter to the Danbury Baptist Association is the origin of the expression "a wall of separation between church and state." It does not appear in the Declaration of Independence or the Constitution.

Eventually, the Supreme Court slowly began to use Jefferson's expression instead of the First Amendment, first in 1878 (*Reynolds v. United States*) and again in 1925 (*Pierce v. Society of Sisters*). It was used for the third time in 1947 (*Everson v. Board of Education*). In that decision, the court proclaimed, "The First Amendment has erected a wall between church and state. That wall must be kept high and impregnable. We could not approve the slightest breach." "Relying on this phrase rather than the First Amendment, courts began striking down religious activities and expressions that had long been constitutional" (Barton, p. 14).

In 1948, in *McCollum v. The Board of Education,* the Supreme Court decided that a voluntary, elective class in religion was unconstitutional. In Illinois, the Champaign Council on Religious Education, consisting of Jews, Roman Catholics, and Protestants, obtained permission from the Board of Education to offer religious instruction classes in grades four through nine. Instructors were approved and supervised by the superintendent of schools. Parents had to give permission for their children to attend. Mrs. Vashti McCollum, an avowed atheist, sued. The Supreme Court declared,

"As we said in the Everson case, the First Amendment has erected a wall between church and state which must be kept high and impregnable" (*McCollum*, 212, cited by Barton, p. 158).

In his *Commentaries on the Constitution,* Supreme Court Justice Joseph Story (1779-1845) said, "The real object of the [First] Amendment was not to countenance much less to advance Mahometanism, or Judaism, or infidelity by prostrating Christianity; but to exclude all rivalry among Christian sects [denominations] and to prevent any national ecclesiastical establishment which should give to a hierarchy [a denominational counsel] the exclusive patronage of the national government" (Story, commentaries on the Constitution of the United States, vol. III, p. 52, cited by Barton, p. 173).

Samuel Adams said, "let ... Statesmen and patriots unite in their endeavor to renovate the age by ... educating little boys and girls ... [and] leading them in the study and practice of the exalted virtues of the Christian system" (from *Four Letters* between Samuel Adams and John Adams, 1802, pp. 9-10, Barton, p. 174).

In 1962, *Engel v. Vitale,* the Supreme Court ruled that the prayer violated the Constitution's establishment clause. The state of New York had a prayer to be read every day at the school opening. It read, "Almighty God, we acknowledge our dependence upon Thee, and we beg Thy blessings upon us, our parents, teachers, and our country. Amen." It was a nonsectarian acknowledgment of God that was called a prayer to whom it may be concerned." Participation was voluntary. The Supreme Court said, "Neither the fact that the prayer may be denominationally neutral nor the fact that its observance on the part of students is voluntary can serve to free it from the limitations of the Establishment Clause, as it might from the Free Exercise Clause, of the First Amendment.... Prayer in its public school system breaches the constitutional wall of separation between church and state (*Engel*, 430, cited by Barton, p. 162). This case was the forerunner of a series of cases that banned any discussion of God from public schools and barred religion from the public square (Horowitz, pp. 49-50).

Engel v. Vitale also stated, "The union of government and religion tends to the destroyed government and to degrade religion" (*Engel*, 431, cited by Barton, p. 162), which is the exact opposite of what virtually all of the Founding Fathers felt. For example, George Washington said, "True religion affords the government its surest support" (*The Writings of George Washington*, vol. XII, pp. 166-167). John Adams said, "Religion and virtue are the only foundations ... of republicanism and of all free governments" (*The Works of John Adams*, vol. IX, p. 636, cited by Barton, p. 162).

In 1963, two cases dealing with Bible reading were combined. In *Murray v. Curlett* (Murray was Madalyn Murray, later Madalyn Murray O'Hair), the Supreme Court banned mandatory reading or recitation of the Bible in public schools. Also, in 1963, in the *School District of Abington Township v. Schempp*, the Supreme Court ruled that mandated Bible reading or prayer in public schools violated the Establishment Clause of the First Amendment. That ruling stated, "The [First] Amendment's purpose was not only to strike merely at the official establishment of a single sect.... It was to create a complete and permanent separation of the spheres of religious activity and civil authority" (*Township* 330, cited by Martin, p. 170).

"After 170 years in which prayers were said and the Bible was read daily in schools across the country, the practice was declared unconstitutional overnight.... Justice Stewart argued that this decision led to 'the establishment of a religion of secularism'" (Horowitz, p. 64).

Benjamin Rush, a signer of the Declaration of Independence, said, "It [the Bible] should be read in our schools in preference to all other books" (Rush, *Essays,* pp. 94, 100, cited by Barton, p. 168). John Jay, the original Chief Justice of the Supreme Court, said, "The Bible is the best of all books, for it is the word of God and teaches us the way to be happy in this world and in the next" (Jay, *The Winning of the Peace, Unpublished Papers* 1780-1784, cited by Barton, p. 168).

In 1979, in *Florey v. Sioux Falls School District,* the Supreme Court concluded that it was "unconstitutional for a kindergarten class to ask whose birthday is celebrated by Christmas" (Barton, p. 19).

In 1980, in *Stone v. Graham,* the Supreme Court ruled that it was unconstitutional for the Ten Commandments to be posted on the walls of public school classrooms. In 1978, Kentucky passed a law requiring the posting of the Ten Commandments in every public school classroom in the state. At the bottom of each poster was printed, "The secular application of the Ten Commandments is clearly seen in its adaptation as the fundamental legal code of Western Civilization and the Common Law of the United States." It was challenged by a group of parents and children representing different religions.

The Supreme Court ruled, "The preeminent purpose for posting the Ten Commandments on the classroom walls is plainly religious in nature. The Ten Commandments are undeniably a sacred text in Jewish and Christian faiths" (*Stone* 41, cited by Barton, p. 176). The Court even said, "If posted copies of the Ten Commandments are to have any effect at all, it will be to introduce the schoolchildren to read, meditate upon, perhaps to venerate and obey, the Commandments" (*Stone* 42, cited by Barton, p. 178).

After pointing out that in another case, Chief Justice Warren

Burger noted, "The very chamber in which oral arguments on this case were heard is decorated with a notable and permanent—not seasonal—symbol of religion: Moses and the Ten Commandments," Barton added, "Perhaps the court had also forgotten that it is often easier to find the Ten Commandments displayed in government rather than religious structures" (Barton, p, 177). Supreme Court Justice William Rehnquist (1924-2005), who wrote the dissent in this case, said, "One can hardly respect the system of education that would leave the students wholly ignorant of the currents of religious thought that move the world society for a part in which he is being prepared" (*Stone* 449, cited by Barton, p. 181). In 2000, the Kentucky legislature passed a law allowing the posting of the Ten Commandments in public classrooms when incorporated into a historical display.

In 1985, in *Wallace v. Jaeffree*, the Supreme Court decided that an Alabama law permitting one minute "for meditation or voluntary prayer" was unconstitutional. The Supreme Court said, "It is not the activity itself and concerns; it is the purpose of the activity that we shall scrutinize" (*Wallace* 472, cited by Barton, p. 181). The Court "discovered" that the prime sponsor of the Alabama bill explained that the bill was an "effort to return voluntary prayer to our public schools" (*Wallace* 43, 44, cited by Barton, p. 182). So, the Court decided that the bill was "invalid because the sole purpose ... was 'an effort on the part of the state of Alabama to encourage a religious activity'... [It] it is a law respecting the establishment of religion within the meaning of the First Amendment" (*Wallace* 41, 42, cited by Barton, p. 182).

In his dissent, Chief Justice Warren Burger pointed out that the sponsor's statement was well over a year after the statute was enacted. He wrote, "There is not a shred of evidence that the legislature as a whole shared the sponsor's motive or that a majority in either house was even aware of the sponsor's view of the bill when it passed" (*Wallace* 86-87, cited by Barton, p. 182). Since the Founders who prohibited an establishment of religion also encouraged religion, it is clear—contrary to the court's assertion in this case—that the Founders did **not** equate encouraging or endorsing religion as an establishment of it" (Barton, p. 184, bold type his). Chief Justice Burger wrote, "the notion that the Alabama statute is a step toward creating an established church border on, it does not trespass into, the ridiculous" (*Wallace* 472, cited by Barton, p. 184). This case extended the prohibition against the establishment to endorsement.

In 1989, in *Allegheny County v. Pittsburgh ACLU*, the Court ruled that it was unconstitutional for the crčche (the nativity scene) to be displayed on government property. What makes this case interesting is that five years earlier, in *Lynch v. Donnelly* (1984), the Court had upheld the use of a nativity scene. In this case, however, the court reversed itself, declaring that the nativity scene "conveys an endorsement of religion, in violation of the establishment of religion clause in the Federal Constitution's First Amendment" (*Allegheny* 106, cited by Barton, p. 186).

In the same decision, the court ruled that the menorah (a multi-branched Jewish candlestick used to celebrate Hanukkah) did not violate the Establishment Clause. This decision also stated that "the Constitution mandates that the government remain secular" (*Allegheny* 574, cited by Barton, p. 187).

In 1990, in *Roberts v. Madigan*, the Supreme Court determined that it was "unconstitutional for a classroom library to contain books that deal with Christianity or for a teacher to be seen with his personal copy of the Bible at school" (Barton, p. 19).

In 1991, in *Alexander v. The Nacogdoches School District*, the Supreme Court ruled it was "unconstitutional for a speaker to deliver a secular message to public schools if that expert is also publicly known to be a Christian—even if he is a member of the President's Drug Task Force" (Barton, p. 19).

In 1992, in *Lee v. Weisman*, the Supreme Court banned clergy-led prayer at a middle school commencement. Providence, Rhode Island, permitted public high schools and middle school principals to invite clergy to offer invocation and benediction prayers at graduation ceremonies. When a middle school principal invited a rabbi to offer such prayers, a student and her father filed suit. The Court ruled, "It is not enough that government refrained from compelling religious practices: it must not engage in them either" (*Lee* 492, cited by Barton, p. 190). It also said that having the crowds stand when the rabbi prayed was psychological coercion (Barton, p. 193) and that public prayers were disruptive and divisive (Barton, p. 194). In 2000, in *Santa Fe ISD v. Doe*, the Supreme Court expanded the ban to include school-organized, student-led prayer at high school football games (Horowitz, pp. 54-55).

In 2006, *Skoros v. City of New York* ruled that it was "constitutional for public schools to display Jewish and Islamic religious holiday symbols but not Christian ones" (Barton, p. 19).

By reinterpreting the First Amendment and misapplying the Fourteenth Amendment, the Supreme Court has eradicated any reference to God, the Bible, and Christianity from public schools.

The Result In contrast to the way the educational system in the U.S. began, today, in the public school system, any mention of God is omitted, and any reference to the Bible is not only eliminated, but things are also taught that are opposed to Scripture, such as the theory of evolution.

God has been edited out of history textbooks in public schools (Horowitz, p. 66). For example, in 2002, the New Jersey Department of Education removed references to the Pilgrims and the Mayflower from school textbooks. Some school systems referred to the Pilgrims merely as "early settlers," "newcomers," or "European colonizers" (Horowitz, p. 57).

The subtitle of the 1987 book *The Closing of the American Mind* is "How Higher Education Has Failed Democracy and Impoverished the Souls of Today's Students." Bloom, a professor of social thought at the University of Chicago, declares that since young people lack an understanding of the past and a vision of the future, they live in an impoverished present.

Paglia, the professor who is an atheist, feminist, and transgender, "recalls a 'horrifying' example from her classroom a few years ago. She was teaching 'Go Down, Moses,' the famous Negro spiritual. 'The whole thing is about antiquity,' she says, 'but obviously, it has contemporary political references.' She passed out the lyrics and played the music, 'and it suddenly hit me with horror—none of them recognized the name 'Moses.' And I thought: Oh my God, when Moses is erased from the West, what is left of Western civilization?'" (from Varadarajan's article in *The Wall Street Journal*, Aug. 30, 2019). The author of that article adds, "Today's college students seem better versed in the polemics of gender identity than in Judeo-Christian history."

In 2001, a Gallup poll of college seniors revealed that 40% did not know when the Civil War occurred (Bruce, p. 178). Non-Christian lesbian Bruce says that the result is students are not learning that the "country [was] based on faith in God, expecting the best of a virtuous people" (Bruce, p. 186). In 2002, three-quarters of college seniors polled "reported that their professors taught them what is right and wrong depends on the differences in individual values and cultural diversity (Bruce, p. 169). In her 2003 book, Bruce says that the academic world is "committed to producing white male graduates who believe that they are the 'racist, sexist, homophobic, oppressor'" (Bruce, p. 189). That may not have been widely known in 2003, but now white men are apologizing for being white males.

By the end of the 20th century, the United States was ranked No.1 in high school and college education, but in 2009, the United States was ranked 18th out of 36 industrialized countries. (www.historynet.com/was-the-usa-ever-no-1-in education?).

Today, in the U.S., in public education, God, the Bible, and Christianity are dead, buried, and forgotten.

Drifting away from Capitalism

Since the founding of the U.S. in 1776, various economic theories have been proposed. A major issue in economic theories is the relationship between the economy and government spending.

Adam Smith On one end of an economic continuum is laissez-faire. The origin of the expression Laissez-faire (French: "leave alone") is uncertain, but a common suggestion is that it originated in the 18th century when Jean-Baptiste Colbert, comptroller general of finance under King Louis XIV of France, asked industrialists what the government could do to help business. They replied, "Leave us alone." Laissez-faire is the separation of economy and state.

Laissez-faire is often associated with capitalism and Adam Smith's *Wealth of Nations* (1776). Smith (1723-1790) was a British economist who is sometimes called the "father of capitalism." Capitalism is sometimes referred to as "Laissez-faire capitalism," but some would say that due to the nature of capitalism, the expression "Laissez-faire Capitalism" is redundant. At any rate, as far as capitalism is concerned, government involvement in the economy should be limited. The government should only intervene to protect the free market, maintain a level playing field, or prevent the unfair advantages of monopolies or oligarchies. In other words, "that government is best which governs least," a quotation often attributed to Thomas Jefferson but was most famously quoted by Henry David Thoreau (1817-1862) in his essay "Civil Disobedience." It is the sentiment that the government should only do what is necessary. It should not intervene in the lives of its citizens unless absolutely necessary.

Karl Marx Karl Marx (1818-1883) formulated the doctrines of "scientific socialism," claiming he discovered "laws" within social structures that produced the inevitable advance of socialism. He called this set of laws the "socialist world revolution." In 1848, Marx and his friend Frederick Engels anonymously wrote the *Communist Manifesto*. According to the *Manifesto*, all of the cruelties of history were caused by the struggle between the *bourgeoisie* (capitalists, the owners of the means of production and employers of wage labor) and the *proletariat* (wage laborers who have no means of production and are forced to sell their labor to live). The steps to revolutionizing the mode of production include 1) the abolition of property and application of all land to public purposes, 2) a progressive income tax, 3) the abolition of all inheritance, 4) confiscation of property of all immigrants and rebels, 5) centralization of credit in the hands of the state by means of a national bank with an exclusivemonopoly, 6) centralization of the means of communication and transportation in the hands of the state,

7) state ownership of factories and instruments of production, 8) the equal liability of all labor, the establishment of industrial armies, especially for agriculture, 9) a more equitable distribution of the population throughout the country, 10) free education for all children in public school.

The *Manifesto* states, "When, in the course of development, class distinctions have disappeared, and all production has been consecrated in the hands of a vast association of the whole nation, the public power will lose its political character." It also says that the proletariat will make itself the ruling class using revolution. It concludes, "They [the communists] openly declared that their ends can be attained only by the forcible overthrow of all existing social conditions. Let the ruling classes tremble at the Communist revolution. The *proletarians* have nothing to lose but their chains. They have a world to win! Workingmen of all countries, unite!"

In short, for Marx, the problem is capitalism, which results in inequality and conflict between the classes. The bourgeoisie conflicts with the proletariat. The solution is a classless society.

On the economic spectrum, capitalism is on one end, and socialism is on the other. They are the exact opposite of each other. Capitalism is concerned with the creation of wealth and socialism is focused on the redistribution of wealth.

Socialism is anti-religion. Dennis Prager observes, "The Marxist worldview is based on a materialist understanding of life. 'Materialism' means that the only reality is matter, that there is no reality beyond the material world. Because religious people have values that transcend the material, Marx called religion the opiate of the masses: It keeps the masses from making social revolution by keeping them happy with non-material concerns and non-material rewards" (Prager, "The Case for Judeo-Christian Values VI").

Socialism limits liberty. The control of the government is in the hands of a few. In a letter he wrote in 1887, John Dalberg-Acton (1834-1902), a.k.a. Lord Acton, a British historian, said, "Power tends to corrupt; absolute power corrupts absolutely. Great men are almost always bad men." As has also been said, "As a person's power increases, their moral sense diminishes."

Socialism kills incentive. "An economics professor dramatically illustrated the fallacy of the redistribution of wealth. He had never failed a single student before but once failed an entire class. That class had insisted that socialism worked and no one would be poor or rich. The professor said, 'OK, we will have an experiment in this class. All grades would be averaged and everyone would receive the same grade so no one would fail and no one would receive an A. The grades were averaged after the first test, and everyone got a B. The students who studied hard were upset and the students who studied little were happy.'

"As the second test rolled around, the students who studied little had studied even less and the ones who studied hard decided they wanted a free ride too, so they studied little. The second test average was a D! No one was happy. When the third test rolled around, the average was an F. The scores never increased as bickering, blame, and name-calling all resulted in hard feelings and no one would study for the benefit of anyone else. All failed, to their great surprise, and the professor told them that socialism would also ultimately fail because when the reward is great, the effort to succeed is great, but when the government takes all the reward away, no one will try or want to succeed. It could not be any simpler than that. As the late [pastor] Adrian Rogers said, 'You cannot multiply wealth by dividing it'" ("Who Is Karl Marx?" by Paul Kengor, Professor of Political Science at Grove City College, posted at Prager University).

There are other problems, such as corruption. When Romania was still under communism behind the Iron Curtain, I traveled there to preach in a renegade Baptist Church. I saw firsthand what communism does. I saw older women sweeping the streets with a straw broom. Building construction was unbelievably poor. Instead of the bricks in the building being constructed in a straight line, there were obvious irregularities in the laying of the bricks so that they looked like they were in waves. I was told about the corruption throughout society. For example, a man walked into a shoe store to buy a pair of shoes. There were only three styles available. When he picked one, he was told that they were out of that particular shoe in his size. When he offered the clerk a bribe, the clerk suddenly remembered that one pair was left in the back.

John Maynard Keynes The Great Depression created a great problem: unemployment. The economic theory of the time held that in the short to medium term, free markets would automatically produce full employment as long as workers were flexible in their wage demands, but during the Depression, that theory did not work. In 1936, John Maynard Keynes (1883-1946) wrote *The General Theory of Employment, Interest, and Money*. He argued that the total spending in the economy (aggregate demand) determines the level of economic activity and that the lack of spending could lead to prolonged periods of high unemployment. He advocated the use of fiscal and monetary policies to mitigate the adverse effects of economic recessions and depressions and "to create a high level of employment and an ongoing profitable economy, without state ownership and without overall state control of the economy" (Muller, p. 118).

In other words, government investment was the golden panacea. "He preached that the major responsibility of government was to create full employment even if it had to borrow money and assume mounting debt to do so (Breese, p. 195). Breese says that Keynes' philosophy can be summed up in the maxim: "The government has all the answers." Breese goes on to say, "Keynes thought he had proved that government intervention would move the economy; government guarantees would stabilize the banks; government protection would satisfy the labor unions; government regulations would stabilize transportation, travel, the media, housing, mortgages, pension funds, and retirement plans; and a thousand other things in which government is now called upon to put produce stability" (Breese, p. 196). Breese concludes, "The government is God! That is Keynesian economics. Keynesian economics also includes the idea that once the crisis is over, government spending would not be as needed."

In the years following the publication of Keynes's book, virtually all capitalist governments adopted Keynes's recommendations. His influence, however, waned in the 1970s, but the global financial crisis of 2007–2008 sparked a resurgence in Keynesian thought. Keynesian economics provided the theoretical underpinning for the economic policies of Barack Obama of the U.S., Prime Minister Gordon Brown of the U.K., and other heads of government. In 1999, when *Time* magazine designated Keynes as one of the most important people of the century, it said, "His radical idea that government should spend money they didn't have may have saved capitalism."

The neo-Keynesian theory argues that the market is not self-regulating and focuses on economic growth and stability rather than full employment.

Milton Friedman In 1962, Milton Friedman (1912-2006) wrote *Capitalism and Freedom*. He challenged what he called "naive Keynesian' theory. He disputed the ability of *government* to favorably regulate the business cycle with fiscal policy and promoted an alternative macroeconomic viewpoint known as "monetarism." He argued that a steady, small expansion of the money supply was the preferred policy. His political philosophy extolled the virtues of a free-market economic system with minimal intervention.

Monetarism argues that excessive money supply expansion is inherently inflationary and that monetary authorities should focus solely on maintaining price stability. The chief method of stabilizing the economy is for a *governing body* to control the money supply by decreasing bond prices and increasing interest rates.

Friedman's ideas concerning monetary policy, taxation, privatization, and deregulation influenced government policies, especially during the 1980s. He was an advisor to Ronald Reagan and Margaret Thatcher. His monetary theory influenced the Federal Reserve's response to the global financial crisis of 2007 and 2008.

To sum up, the modern economic theories are capitalism (some government regulation), socialism (government ownership), and Keynesian economics (government spending) and Monetarism (a governing body controlling money supply). Marx decided Marxism would solve the problems of inequality and class struggle. Keynes developed Keynesian economics because of unemployment. Friedman designed monetarism to address inflation.

The Bible As we have seen, the Bible supports certain concepts of capitalism, the private ownership of property, the accumulation of wealth, and making money by the use of money. What does the Bible say about the relationship between government and economics? The Bible approves of the government collecting taxes (Mark 12:17-17), but what does it say about how the government should spend the money? The function of government is to regulate society by the rule of law (Exodus 20 ff.). According to the New Testament, government is God's institution to punish evil and praise good (Romans 13:3-4).

That is their job. Therefore, believers should pay taxes to enable them to do that (Romans 13:6). In its God-given responsibility of punishing evil and praising good, the government's role in economics would be to serve as an umpire to make sure that the players play fair. For example, the government should pass laws to prevent unfair business practices such as monopolies. No doubt, the government has to provide for the national defense.

What about welfare? For starters, the Bible recognizes that there will always be poor people (Deuteronomy 15:11; Matthew 26:11). Charles Murray (MIT, Ph.D. in Political Science) points out that "poverty has been the condition of the vast majority of human community since the dawn of history, and they have for the most part been communities of stable families, mature children, and low crime" (Murray in the Preface to Olasky's *The Tragedy of American Compassion*, p. xiii).

The Bible divides those in need into two groups. Some people have needs through no fault of their own, such as orphans and widows (James 1:27). Others are able to work but for some reason do not (2 Thessalonians 3:10). Paul says, "If anyone will not work, neither shall he eat" (2 Thessalonians 3:10). Who is to care for those who have legitimate needs through no fault of their own?

In the first place, the Bible teaches it is the family's responsibility to take care of family members. When the *family* functions as God intended, which includes the extended family, people grow up to be responsible, functioning individuals. Those within a family with legitimate needs are to be cared for by the family. Paul says, "If any widow has children or grandchildren, let them first learn to show piety at home and to repay their parents; but this is good and acceptable before God" (1 Timothy 5:4; see also 5:16). Believers do not provide for their own they have denied the faith and no worse than an unbeliever (1 Timothy 5:8).

In the second place, beyond family relationships, people are to take care of one another. The answer to Cain's question, "Am I my brother's keeper?" is yes (Genesis 4:9). If a family or a nation is to survive, people must be responsible for the well-being of one another. Moses said we are to love our neighbors as ourselves (Leviticus 19:18) and expands that to include resident aliens (Leviticus 19:34; see Deuteronomy 15:7, 11; Proverbs 22:9). According to Jesus, the second greatest commandment (Matthew 22:39) is we should love our neighbor as ourselves (Leviticus 19:18, a verse which is quoted in the New Testament more than any other Old Testament verse). When Jesus was asked, "who is my neighbor?" Jesus told the parable of the good Samaritan (Luke 10:29-36), which essentially means your neighbor is anyone whose need you see, whose need you can meet (from a sermon by Haddon Robinson). Today, this would include private charitable organizations.

In the third place, under some circumstances, if there is no family, it is the responsibility of the *church* to care for some widows but not all widows in the church. To be financially supported by the church, a widow must have some qualifications (1 Timothy 5:3-16).

So, how does the government fit into all of this? There is nothing in the Bible about *government* taking care of people. The Bible does not sanction anybody, government, or individuals, giving money to people who are able to work but don't. Paul emphatically stated, "If anyone will not work, neither shall he eat" (2 Thessalonians 3:11). The Bible does not even say anything about the government taking care of orphans and widows. It does not support the idea that the government should tax the rich to help the poor. In January 1794, during a debate in the House of Representatives for relief of St. Domingo refugees, James Madison said, "Charity is no part of the legislative duty of the government." Breese says, "In the economy of God, the government has never been appointed to be the father, mother, the rich uncle, the provider, or the Savior of each one of its individual people" (Breese, p. 200). The Keynesian view that government can do it all is not biblical.

So, from a biblical perspective, ideally, those in need should be cared for by the family, in some cases, the church, and by neighbor taking care of neighbor. It has been suggested that Jesus would prefer that people give their money to the Salvation Army to help the poor rather than being taxed by the politicians to fund a welfare bureaucracy (https://www.prageru.com/video/was-jesus-a-socialist/).

The more the government does to help people (welfare), the less responsible they become and the less compassionate people become. If the U.S. returned to the biblical system of families taking care of family members, the church assisting in some cases, and neighbors caring about neighbors, people would become more responsible and compassionate.

The American Experience In *The Tragedy of American Compassion*, Olasky describes poverty-fighting in America from colonial times to the 1990s. He argues that current government welfare programs are ineffective because they are disconnected from the poor and that private programs are more effective in changing lives because the people in them have a personal connection with the recipient. As Murray says in the Preface to the book, in past American history, "Human needs were answered by other human beings, not by bureaucrats, and the response of those needs was not compartmentalized. People didn't use to be so foolish as to think that providing food would cure anything except hunger, not so shallow as to think that physical hunger is more important than other human hunger, or so blind as to ignore the interaction between the *way* one helps in the efforts of that help on the human spirit and human behavior " (Murray, in Olasky, p. xv). I highly recommend reading this eye-opening book.

According to Milton Friedman, the closest anyone has ever come to a capitalist system was the U.S. in the 19th century. The federal government spent roughly 3% of the national income on the Army and Navy. States and local governments spent approximately 6-7% of the national income mainly on schooling. Very little was spent on welfare programs. It was during this time that there was the greatest voluntary charitable activity in this country or any other at any time (Friedman, "Is Capitalism Humane?" at 37:14-38:7 ff.; https://www.youtube.com/watch?v=27Tf8RN3uiM).

The welfare system is based on Keynesian economics. While the welfare system has helped some, it has also killed people's dignity. Even the radical Saul D. Alinsky, who dedicated *Rules for Radicals* to Lucifer, "the first radical known to man who rebelled against the establishment and did it so effectively that he at least won his own kingdom," argues that people must have dignity and that dignity is obtained by them when they participate. To illustrate his point, he says, "In *Reveille for Radicals,* I described an incident in which the government of Mexico once decided to pay tribute to Mexican mothers. A proclamation was issued that every mother whose sewing machine was being held by the Monte de Piedad (the national pawnshop of Mexico) should have her machine returned as a gift on Mother's Day. There was tremendous joy over the occasion. Here was a gift being made outright, without any participation on the part of the recipients. Within three weeks, the same number of sewing machines was back in the pawnshop" (Alinsky, pp. 123-124). That giveaway program did not produce more work and, therefore, more dignity through accomplishment.

Years ago, when I was preaching in Alaska, a missionary told me of visiting a village of Eskimos, where all the people received government assistance to such an extent that they did not have to work. As a result, every man, woman, and child in the village was drunk. When the government provides people's needs, they lose dignity, incentive, and motivation to work.

The Results Today, the current U.S. government's economic policies based on the Keynesian notion that the government should borrow money and assume mounting debt has resulted in a drift away from capitalism toward socialism, the creation of massive government welfare programs, and enormous, mind-boggling debt. As of April 1, 2023, the United States government has accumulated over $31 trillion in debt, a figure so high we can't even imagine what it means (for the up-to-the-minute amount, see https://www.usdebtclock.org).

Deserting the Rule of Law

The Judicial Branch Thomas Jefferson worried that the Courts would overstep their authority and, instead of interpreting the law, would begin making law. He said, "The Constitution is a mere thing of wax in the hands of the judiciary, which they may twist and shape into any form they please" (Jefferson, cited by Federer, p. 330). Sure enough, courts today practice judicial fiat over democratic decision-making. Activist judges are virtually making laws.

In 1994, California Proposition 187 was approved by 59% to 41%. It denied government services to illegal aliens. It won in every county in the state of California except San Francisco. Then, District Court Judge Mariana Pfaelzer held that Proposition 187 was "unconstitutional." So, California taxpayers pay for food, housing, education, and health care for illegal immigrants. In 2008, Californians voted 52% to 48% against gay marriage. Again, a district court judge overturned the vote.

When the Supreme Court made same-sex marriage a constitutional right, it bypassed the Constitution and Congress, whose right is to make laws. In an article entitled "Who Let the Supreme Court Make Laws?" (April 14, 2017), Gil Troy wrote, "Shouldn't the Congress and the president have boldly passed a law or constitutional amendment authorizing gay marriage? It is unfortunate that gay marriage entered into legal legitimacy through the slippery Supreme Court backdoor rather than through the more democratic, populist front door" (see the article at https://www.thedailybeast.com/who-let-the-supreme-court-make-laws?ref=scroll).

The Executive Branch Members of the executive branch have also deserted the rule of law. As a result of a break-in at the Watergate Hotel in Washington DC to steal information from the Democrat party, in July 1974, a congressional committee approved three articles of impeachment against President Richard Nixon (obstruction of justice, abuse of power, and contempt of Congress) and reported those articles to the House of Representatives for a vote. In response, Richard Nixon resigned.

The Obama administration made a nuclear deal with Iran, which should have been presented to Congress as a treaty that would acquire a two-thirds majority in the Senate to take effect. Secretary of State John Kerry told the House Foreign Affairs Committee that the deal wasn't a treaty simply because "You can't pass a treaty anymore." In an article that appeared in the *Orange County Register* entitled "The long, slow death of the rule of law in America" (August 27, 2015), Troy Senik wrote, "This is a wholesale abandonment of the foundational American principle of the rule of law."

Senik added, "There are only two options available here: Either the country returns to a form of government bound by the strictures of the Constitution and its subordinate laws or we give up the ghost and accept the fact that our politics are now entirely about power rather than principle–that we live in a nation where the president, whether his name is Obama or Trump, is limited only by the boundaries of imagination. There are a lot of ways to describe that form of government. 'Constitutional republic' isn't one of them."

James Madison said, "The truth is that all men having power ought to be mistrusted." Now, there is a biblical idea (Psalm 118:8-9). That is why checks and balances are needed in government and why the three branches not staying in their lane is serious.

The Result Lawlessness is loose in our land. America has moved from the land of law to a land of lawlessness, from a land of doing what is right because it's right to a land of doing what feels good. In his 1932 book about the art of bullfighting titled *Death in the Afternoon*, Ernest Hemingway wrote, "What is moral is what you feel good after and what is immoral is what you feel bad after." The English historian and philosopher Arnold Toynbee (1889-1975) said that we are the first generation of man to try to build a society without a moral reference point.

Bruce laments that the results are seen "with judges or juries failing to impose death sentences on cop killers, dropping charges against a woman who murdered her own child, freeing violent men on parole, taking a lenient and sometimes even sympathetic view of child molesters, giving more rights to convicts than to law-abiding citizens, and, now, holding a man whose property was stolen and the company who had sold the stolen property responsible for the use the thief made of it" (Bruce, p. 264).

Cities declaring themselves "sanctuary cities" are refusing to obey federal laws. The government gives drug addicts needles. "The city of San Francisco handed out a total of 5.8 million free syringes to drug addicts in 2018" (Michael Snyder; see bibliography for details). In 2020, rioters and looters repeatedly broke into stores, stole merchandise, and destroyed property without interference from the police.

Today, in the U.S., in too many cases, the rule of law is virtually dead in many cases.

Destroying Life

Abortion "The Supreme Court did not 'invent' legal abortion, much less abortion itself, when it handed down its historic *Roe v. Wade* decision in 1973. Abortion, both legal and illegal, had long been part of life in America. Indeed, the legal status of abortion has passed through several distinct phases in American history. Generally permitted at the nation's founding and for several decades after that, the procedure was made illegal under most circumstances in most states beginning in the mid-1800s. In the 1960s, states began reforming their strict antiabortion laws so that when the Supreme Court made abortion legal nationwide, legal abortions were already available in 17 states under a range of circumstances beyond those necessary to save a woman's life" (https://www.guttmacher.org/gpr/2003/03/lessons-roe-will-past-be-prologue#)

In 1967, Colorado Governor John A. Love signed the first liberalized abortion law in the U.S., which allowed abortion in cases of permanent mental or physical disability of either the child or mother or in cases of rape or incest. Similar laws were passed in

California, Oregon, and North Carolina. In 1970, New York allowed abortion on demand up to the 24th week of pregnancy. In 1971, the U.S. Supreme Court ruled on its first abortion case (*United States v. Vuitch*). It upheld the District of Columbia law permitting abortion only to preserve a woman's life or "health." The court, however, made it clear that by "health," it meant "psychological and physical well-being, effectively allowing abortion for any reason.

In 1973, the U.S. Supreme Court issued a ruling in *Roe v. Wade* that said a "right of privacy" was "broad enough to encompass" a right to abortion. That ruling also provided guidelines for the states, dividing pregnancy into three 12-week trimesters. A state could enact virtually no restriction on abortion in the first trimester. A state could enact some regulation in the second trimester, but only to protect maternal "health." A state could ostensibly "proscribe" abortion in the third trimester. During the third trimester, the state's interest in protecting the potential human life outweighs the woman's right to privacy. The state may prohibit abortions unless an abortion is necessary to save the life or health of the mother. In 1992, in *Planned Parenthood v. Casey*, the Supreme Court discarded the trimester scheme.

On the same day, the Supreme Court issued a ruling in *Roe v. Wade*, it also ruled in *Doe v. Bolton* that "health" means "all factors" that affect the woman, including "physical, emotional, psychological, familial, and the woman's age."

In 1976, the Supreme Court ruled in *Planned Parenthood of Central Missouri v. Danforth*, against a parental consent requirement and decided that (married) fathers had no rights in the abortion decision. In the same year, the Massachusetts Superior Judicial Court overturned the manslaughter conviction of an abortionist, saying that legal abortions are only manslaughter if the baby is definitely alive outside the mother's body. In 1981, the Supreme Court in *H.L. v. Matheson*, upheld a Utah parental notification law, which required an abortionist to notify the parents of a minor girl who is still living at home as her parent's dependent when an abortion is scheduled.

In 1983, in *Akron v. Akron Center for Reproductive Health*, the Supreme Court struck down state requirements that abortions performed after the first trimester be done in a hospital, women's right to know laws, and waiting periods after information is provided to the woman seeking an abortion before she can consent to an abortion.

In 1995, Congress passed the Partial-Birth Abortion Ban Act. "Partial-birth abortion" involves the abortionist delivering all but the head of a baby from her mother's womb, piercing the skull, and suctioning out the brain, then completing the delivery. President Clinton vetoed the bill. In 1997, Ron Fitzsimmons, head of the National Coalition of Abortion Providers, told journalists he "lied through my teeth" in claiming that partial-birth abortions were performed very rarely and only for extraordinary medical reasons, explaining that he had just "spouted the party line" developed by leaders of other pro-abortion groups.

Infanticide On the program "Ask the Governor," aired on January 30, 2019, Virginia Governor Ralph Northam (1959-) defended the Repeal Act. This abortion bill would remove the requirement that three physicians agree that a woman needs a late-term abortion. It would require only the consent of the mother and of the physician performing the abortion. The bill would allow a woman to receive an abortion even while she was going into labor. In the interview, the governor, a former pediatrician, said, "If a mother is in labor, I can tell you exactly what would happen. The infant would be delivered. The infant would be kept comfortable. The infant would be resuscitated if that's what the mother and the family desired, and then a discussion would ensue between the physicians and the mother." That is infanticide!

In response to Northam's comments, Senator Ben Sasse (R., Neb.) said, "This is morally repugnant. In just a few years, pro-abortion zealots went from 'safe, legal, and rare' to 'keep the newborns comfortable while the doctor debates.' I don't care what party you're from—if you can't say that it's wrong to leave babies to die after birth, get the hell out of public office." Later that day, Northam released a statement appearing to walk back his comments. "No woman seeks a third-trimester abortion except in the case of tragic or difficult circumstances, such as a nonviable pregnancy or in the event of severe fetal abnormalities, and the governor's comments were limited to actions physicians would take in the event that a woman in those circumstances went into labor.... Attempts to extrapolate these comments otherwise is in bad faith and underscores exactly why the governor believes physicians and women, not legislators, should make these difficult and deeply personal medical decisions." He made it worse. The killing of an unborn baby is a moral issue.

Peter Singer (1946-), the Oxford-trained DeCamp Professor of Bioethics at Princeton University, believes the moral difference between a human being and a horse is only a matter of degree. He concedes that his "quality of life" ethic explicitly rejects the "sanctity of life" view. He defends infanticide, arguing that parents should have the legal option to kill their newborns up to 28 days after birth!

John Silber (1926-2012), a professor of philosophy and President of Boston University, told a meeting of 3,000 philosophers that Singer was rejecting ultimate truth and the consequent relativizing of all values. After all, our nation is founded upon a conception of man derived from "the laws of nature and nature's God," the same conception enshrined in Latin under the Princeton crest: *Dei Sub Numine Viget* ("We will flourish under the command of God").

The Result The result of rejecting the living God and the truth that people are made in His image is death. Only in an environment that rejects absolute truth and emphasizes individual rights, self-sufficiency, subjectivism, and relativism can abortion be legalized (Foh, p. 40). G. K. Chesterton said, "When people stop believing in God, they don't believe in nothing—they believe in anything."

Since 1970, Dennis Prager has asked high school seniors if they were on a boat and a stranger and their dog were drowning, which one they would try to save first. He says, "Two-thirds have voted against the person" (Dennis Prager, "The Case for Judeo-Christian Values," Part IV).

The Centers for Disease Control and Prevention keep a record of the number of legal induced abortions. The CDC numbers are derived from every abortion reported to state health departments. Reporting to the CDC is not mandatory and some states, including California, do not report abortions to the CDC. According to the CDC records, between 1970 and 2015, there were 45.7 million legally induced abortions in the U.S.

The pro-choice Guttmacher Institute also keeps track of abortions. They consistently identify higher rates of abortion than the CDC. Additionally, they say their numbers underestimate abortion rates by up to five percent. Both pro-choice and pro-life activists consider the Guttmacher figures to be more accurate than the CDC's.

In 2015, the *Des Moines Register* did a fact check on Iowa state Rep. Greg Heartsill, who said there had been 50 million abortions since *Roe v. Wade*. The *Register* reported that the Guttmacher

Institute did show more than 50 million abortions were performed between 1973 and 2011. They added, "Those findings are peer-reviewed and have been cited by proponents and opponents of legal access to abortion alike. Figures compiled by the federal government over the same period show less than 50 million, but are missing data from several states over several years"https://www.desmoinesregister.com/story/news/politics/reality-check/2015/03/06/million-abortions-claim-checks/24530159/, accessed August 22, 2019). For the up-to-the-minute figure, see usabortionclock.org.

Since then, the data shows that abortions are on the decline. In September 2019, the Guttmacher Institute estimated that there were about 862,000 abortions in 2017, nearly 200,000 fewer than in 2011. The abortion rate (the number of abortions per 1,000 women of reproductive age) dropped to 13.5 in 2017 from 16.9 in 2011, the lowest rate since abortion became legal nationwide in 1973. (https://www.nytimes.com/2019/09/18/health/abortion-rate-dropped.html). That is great news, but the reduced number is still bad news.

Abortion is an example of moral relativism. Prager says, "There is no clearer expression of moral relativism: Every woman determines whether abortion is moral. On the other hand, to the individual with Judeo-Christian values, it is not between anyone and anyone else. It is between society and God…. Personal feelings have supplanted universal standards" (Prager, "The Case for Judeo-Christian Values IV").

Today, in the U.S., the rejection of the biblical view of the sanctity of life has resulted in death—literally!

On June 24, 2022, the US Supreme Court overturned Roe v. Wade. Some state constitutions, however, still allow abortions.

Death in the U.S. Society

Summary: Beginning in the latter part of the 19th century and continuing to the present, the society of the U.S. has more and more departed from its original Christian-influenced society by discrediting the Bible, dethroning God, discounting moral responsibility, dumbing-down education, devaluing marriage, drifting away from capitalism, deserting the rule of law, and destroying life with abortion.

Times have changed. Compared to its birth, the original ideals in the U.S. are dead. Today, the Bible is abused by its friends and attacked by its enemies. Christianity is marginalized and mocked. People escape personal responsibility by playing the blame game or by playing the victim. Immorality is rampant. The God-ordained design for marriage between Adam and Eve has been extended to the man-manufactured marriage between Adam and Al or Eve and Esther. The number of children born outside of marriage is 40%. Any trace of God and the Bible in the U.S. educational system has disappeared. Respect for law, authority, and each other is fast fading from the scene. On top of that, there is literal death, deaths from drug addiction, suicide, and mothers scarifying unborn babies on the altar of their choice. Since *Roe v. Wade*, there have been more than 60 million abortions—and counting!

Departure from biblical values such as acknowledging God, personal responsibility and the traditional family has catastrophic consequences. "There is a way that seems right to a man, but its end is the way of death" (Proverbs 14:12; repeated in Proverbs 16:25).

The U.S. society is producing death—literally. Dr. Francie Hart Broghammer, the chief psychiatry resident at UC Irvine Medical Center, says, "Since the turn of the century, Americans have been dying from suicide, alcohol-related illnesses, and drug overdoses at a rate that has never before been seen.... Suicide is now the second-leading cause of death for American teenagers and the tenth-leading cause of death for Americans overall. The suicide rate has increased by more than 30 percent in half of U.S. states since 1999. Equally harrowing, drug overdose is the leading cause of death for Americans under the age of fifty.... In 2017 alone, approximately 47,000 Americans committed suicide, and over 70,000 individuals died of a drug overdose. To put these numbers into perspective, 40,000 Americans died in motor vehicle accidents during that same year, while roughly 58,000 U.S. soldiers died in the Vietnam War as a whole.... Our psychological and spiritual lives are in freefall" (Broghammer, see Bibliography).

Chapter 4

LIFE AFTER DEATH IN THE U.S. SOCIETY

The Christian values and ideals that so penetrated the U.S. society for so many years are dead (or on life support). Simply put, the cause of death is the departure from those ideals. The United States is now in a Post Christian era; it is a *secular society.*

"Secular" denotes attitudes and actions without religious or spiritual basis. In 1983, Aleksandr Solzhenitsyn delivered a speech in London in which he said, "If I were called upon to identify briefly the principal trait of the *entire* twentieth century, here too, I would be unable to find anything more precise and pithy than to repeat once again: Men have forgotten God" (Solzhenitsyn, italics his, http://orthochristian.com/47643.html).

Description Speaking about our now secular society, In his weekly blog, Fred Chay, a theology professor, puts it like this: "The worldview of Atheism rejects the sacred and reduces everything to the secular. It comes through many venues. One source is Romanticism and its resulting Humanism. This led to Scientific Positivism or Darwinian Naturalism. (Nature is the whole show.) This produced the chilling political philosophy of Karl Marx called Materialism. His goal was to eliminate the sacred and reduce everything to the secular or the material. This view reduces everything to physical, material, or trace elements. It results in seeing, according to B. F. Skinner, 'no essential difference between a rat, a radish, or a person.' Atheism has no transcendent objective truth from God, only subjective values that change at the whims of man. Ethics that determine right and wrong or good and bad are replaced with the options of legal or illegal. Morality in a secular world has mutated from its sacred source because 'True Truth' is the casualty in a society devoid of the transcendent Christ" (Fred Chay's Blog, "Friday with Fred"). In other words, theism has been replaced by naturalism, humanism, materialism, etc.

The Means As a result of Supreme Court decisions, the public education system from kindergarten to graduate school, Hollywood, television, music, the news media, the Internet, and social media, the society of the U.S. is now heavily influenced by secularism. According to the Pew Research Center, in 2018, 34% of U.S. adults said they preferred to get news online through websites, apps, or social media. Yet 57% said they expected the news they see on these platforms to be mostly inaccurate (https://www.schwartzreport.net/key-findings-about-the-online-news-landscape-in-america/, accessed November 9, 2019).

Music is particularly influential on young people and some of what popular music teaches is wrong. One example is Ice-T's 1992 song "Cop Killer," celebrating the killing of police officers. Plato observed that musical training is a more potent instrument than any other because rhythm and harmony find their way into the inward places of the soul, on which they mightily fasten. Blaise Pascal observed that the people who have the greatest influence in shaping the hearts and minds of any generation are not the folks who write the laws but those who write the songs.

In the final analysis, values are more caught than taught. When Judeo-Christian values heavily influenced U.S. society, those values were "caught." Now, secular values are not only being taught in the public education system, but they are also part of the society that is being "caught" by young people through exposure to the Internet, music, social media, Hollywood, etc.

The Response One of the interesting verses in the ignored book of 1 Chronicles is 1 Chronicles 12:32, which speaks of "the sons of Issachar ... [who] understood the times to know what Israel ought to do." Now that we understand the times in the U.S., what needs to be done? What should we do? It has been suggested that America is not at a crossroads; it is a long way down the wrong road, and it needs to return to the crossroads and take the right road (Thomas, p. 21). How is that done? Reviewing what happened at the founding of the United States provides insight into what needs to occur now, namely, the Bible was respected, God was acknowledged, and people believed in moral responsibility.

Respect The Bible

To survive and thrive in a secular society, believers in Jesus Christ must "think biblically."

Live Life Remember millions of believers in Jesus Christ for thousands of years, including today, have lived and are living normal lives in pagan societies. Jeremiah sent a letter to all the Judahites who had gone into exile in Babylon in 597 B.C. (Jeremiah 29:1-4). This is like a pastor sending a letter to his former church members who are now living in a non-Christian environment. The first thing he tells them to do is live normal lives. Jeremiah says, "Thus saith the Lord ... 'Build houses and dwell *in them;* plant gardens and eat their fruit. Take wives and beget sons and daughters; and take wives for your sons and give your daughters to husbands, so that they may bear sons and daughters that you may be increased there, and not diminished'" (Jeremiah 29:5-6). Regardless of the values that permeated society, go to work, get married, buy a house, have children, and live a normal life.

Do not be Conformed Believers in Jesus Christ are not to be conformed to this world (Romans 12:2). The Greek word translated "world" means "age." Believers must not be conformed to the latest trends, such as disregarding the Bible and dethroning God. They should not be concerned with the materialism and consumerism that consume the current secular society. Jesus said, "Take heed and beware of covetousness, for one's life does not consist in the abundance of the things he possesses" (Luke 12:15).

The apostle Paul established churches and wrote letters to churches in a secular society. In the process, he described the kind of secular society to which believers should not be conformed. In February 57 AD, Paul wrote to the church in Rome, describing what amounts to a secular society. Suppressing the truth, people lived ungodly and unrighteous lives (Romans 1:18). They change "the glory of the incorruptible God into an image made like corruptible man—and birds and four-footed animals and creeping things" (Romans 1:23). They exchange "the truth of God for the lie" (Romans 1:25). Consequently, they practice homosexuality (Romans 1:26-27), sexual immorality, wickedness, covetousness, maliciousness; [were] full of envy, murder, strife, deceit, evil-mindedness; *they are* whisperers, backbiters, haters of God, violent, proud, boasters, inventors of evil things, disobedient to parents, undiscerning, untrustworthy, unloving, unforgiving, unmerciful" (Romans 1:29-31).

As pointed out, "Ships do not sink because of the water around them. Ships sink because of the water that gets inside of them. The moral of the story is don't let what is happening around you get inside of you and weigh you down." In short, do not be conformed to this age.

Be Conformed As God's children, believers are to be God-like. The Old Testament emphasizes that God is holy (Leviticus 11:44) and the New Testament stresses that God is love (1 John 4:8). Around holiness can be grouped such attributes as truth, righteousness, and justice; clustered with love are grace, mercy, and kindness. Thus, the two major characteristics of God are holiness (truth, righteousness, justice) and love (grace, mercy, kindness). Micah says, "He has shown you, O man, what *is* good; and what does the LORD require of you but to do justly, to love mercy, and to walk humbly with your God?" (Micah 6:8).

Believers in Jesus Christ are "to be conformed to the image of His Son" (Romans 8:29). Jesus was full of grace and truth (John 1:14). Jesus says, "Woe to you, scribes and Pharisees, hypocrites! For you pay tithe of mint and anise and cummin and have neglected the weightier *matters* of the law: justice and mercy and faith. These you ought to have done, without leaving the others undone" (Mt. 23:23).

Paul says, "But, speaking the truth in love, (you) may grow up in all things into Him who is the head—Christ" (Eph. 4:15). Just speaking the truth is not the issue. Believers are to speak the truth in love. A lady once told Winston Churchill, "You are drunk." Churchill replied, "You are ugly, but I will wake up sober in the morning." That is speaking the truth but not speaking the truth in love. Churchill was not seeking her highest good, the definition of agape love. It was a put-down.

To have Christ-like maturity, believers must be righteous (Hebrews 5:13) and loving (Ephesians 4:15). Paul says, "But you, O man of God, flee these things and pursue righteousness, godliness, faith, love, patience, gentleness" (1 Timothy 6:11) and "Flee also youthful lusts; but pursue righteousness, faith, love, peace with those who call on the Lord out of a pure heart" (2 Timothy 2:22). When Paul sums up the spiritual qualities to be pursued, he mentions different attributes in these two lists, but the two characteristics that are the same in both lists are righteousness and love.

Attend a Bible Teaching Church As pointed out earlier, Bill Petro goes so far as to say that sermons were one of the causes of the Revolution. He says, "Clergy molded public opinion by political sermons." The greatest need in America today is for America to get back to the Bible. "Where *there is* no revelation, the people cast off restraint; but happy *is* he who keeps the law" (Proverbs 29:18). In this proverb, "revelation" means the Word of God." First Samuel 3:1 says, "The word of the LORD was rare in those days; *there was* no widespread revelation." In other words, this proverb is about not having the Word of God. When the Word of God is not known, people cast off restraint. On the other hand, those individuals who keep the law, that is, obey God's Word, are happy (see Psalm 1:1-2, where "blessed" means "happy"). Public morality and personal happiness are dependent on obedience to the Word of God and trust in the God of the Word.

Benjamin Franklin said, "Whoever shall introduce into public affairs the principles of primitive Christianity will change the face of the world" (Federer, p. 246). Noah Webster (1758-1843), called the "Father of American Scholarship and Education, said, "The moral principles and precepts contained in the scriptures ought to form the basis of all our civil constitutions and laws…. All the miseries and evils which men suffer from vice, crime, ambition, injustice, oppression, slavery, and war proceed from their despising or neglecting the precepts contained in the Bible." Alexis de Tocqueville

(1805-1859) said, "Liberty cannot be established without morality, nor morality without faith."

One of the greatest needs in America today is for pastors to teach the Word of God. One of the most important elements in the formation of the United States was the widespread preaching from the pulpits of the colonies. Less than 50% of the people in the U.S. are Protestants as compared to 98% in 1776, but not all Protestants today believe the Bible is the Word of God. May the Lord raise up Bible-teaching churches. That is not an impossible dream. He can do that.

Lead People to Christ This secular society has produced the idea that government can solve our problems. These problems are people problems. *People* have to change. In his book *Dark Agenda,* David Horowitz says injustice is not caused by society, oppressive races, genders, or solely by our political enemies. "Injustice is the result of human selfishness, deceitfulness, malice, envy, greed, and lust. Injustice is the inevitable consequence of our free will as human beings. 'Society' is not the cause of injustice. Society is merely a reflection of who we are" (Horowitz, p. 33).

In other words, if the situation is to be changed, *people need to be changed*, and the gospel of Jesus Christ changes people. The way to change society is not from the top down but from the bottom up or, better yet, from the inside out. Many years ago, evangelist Lester Roloff said, "If America is to be saved, we must save Americans" and the pastor of a large church said, "The issue is not who is in the White House; it is who is in the Father's house."

Rely on The Lord

Salvation As was pointed out in the first chapter, Jesus Christ died for our sins and rose from the dead (1 Corinthians 15:3-5). When people trust Jesus Christ for the gift of eternal life (John 3:16; 1 Timothy 1:16), they are guaranteed eternal life (John 5:24). This trust in Jesus Christ is reliance upon Him and Him alone, not anything we do (Ephesians 2:8-9) to obtain the forgiveness of sins now (Acts 13:39) and a home in heaven later (John 14:1-6).

Spiritual Growth Believers are to grow in the grace and knowledge of Jesus Christ (2 Peter 3:18). That is done by obeying God's Word (John 13:34-35) by depending on the Lord for the strength to do that (Philippians 3:10). In other words, we live by faith (Galatians 2:20), by relying on the Lord. "Let us, therefore, come boldly to the throne of grace, that we may obtain mercy and find grace to help in time of need" (Hebrews 4:16).

Pray Jeremiah wrote to Judahites in exile in Babylon to tell them that the Lord said, "And seek the peace of the city where I have caused you to be carried away captive, and pray to the LORD for it; for in its peace you will have peace" (Jeremiah 29:7). The exiles in Babylon were to *seek the peace of the city* where they lived, including praying for peace because when the city had peace, they would have peace. In the current situation, that will be praying for more civility.

Paul said, "Therefore I exhort first of all that supplications, prayers, intercessions, *and* giving of thanks be made for all men, for kings and all who are in authority, that we may lead a quiet and peaceable life in all godliness and reverence. For this *is* good and acceptable in the sight of God our Savior" (1 Timothy 2:1-3). We are to pray for leaders that *we* (not just them) may lead a peaceable life in godliness and reverence. Pray for all that are in authority, leaders on a national, state, and local level, that they will make just, merciful, and wise (Psalm 101:1-2). Decisions that will promote peace.

The prayer list should also include the things that would put the ship of state back on the course set by the Founding Fathers. The most important things needed in America today are a return to shepherds teaching the Word of God in churches, traditional families teaching the Bible to their children, and the education system exposing students to moral responsibility.

The ultimate answer is not political; it is prayer. In June 1787, the Constitutional Convention in Philadelphia was embroiled in a bitter debate over how the state would be represented in the new government. The smaller states were pitted against the larger states. The contention was so great that some delegates left the Convention. On Thursday, June 28, 1787, 81-year-old Benjamin Franklin rose to speak. James Madison, who kept meticulous personal notes of the convention's events and debates, recorded Franklin's speech.

Benjamin Franklin declared, "In this situation of this assembly, groping as it were in the dark to find political truth, and scarce able to distinguish it when presented to us, how has it happened, Sir, that we have not hitherto once thought of humbly applying to the Father of lights, to illuminate our understanding? In the beginning of the contest with G. Britain, when we were sensible of danger, we had daily prayer in this room for Divine protection. Our prayers, Sir, were heard, & they were graciously answered. All of us who were engaged in the struggle must have observed frequent instances of superintending Providence in our favor.

"To that kind of Providence, we owe this happy opportunity to consult in peace on the means of establishing our future national felicity. And have we now forgotten that powerful friend? Or do we imagine we no longer need his assistance? I have lived, Sir, a long time and the longer I live, the more convincing proofs I see of this truth—that God governs in the affairs of men. And if a sparrow cannot fall to the ground without his notice, is it probable that an empire can rise without his assistance? We have been assured, sir, in the sacred writings, that 'except the Lord build the house, they labor in vain that build it.' I firmly believe this, and I also believe that without his concurring aid we shall succeed in this political building no better than the builders of Babel. We should be divided by our partial local interests; our projects will be confounded, and we ourselves to become a reproach in a byword down to future ages. And what is worse, mankind may hereafter, from this unfortunate incident, despair of establishing government by human wisdom and leave it to chance, war and conquest."

"I, therefore, bag leave to move—that henceforth prayers imploringly assistance of heaven, and its blessing on our deliberation, be held in this assembly every morning before we proceed to business and that one or more of the clergy of the city be requested to officiate in that service" (printed in *Papers of James Madison*, Henry D. Gilpin, editor, 1840, vol. II, pp, 984-986, June 28, 1787, cited by Federer, pp. 248-249; Barton, pp. 116-117).

James Madison moved that Franklin's appeal for prayer be enacted and Edmund Jennings Randolph further moved "that a sermon be preached at the request of the convention on the 4th of July, the anniversary of independence; & henceforward prayers be used in ye convention every morning." Prayers have opened both houses of Congress ever since (Federer, p. 249).

When the Convention reconvened on July 2, 1787, Jonathan Dayton recorded, "Every unfriendly feeling had been expelled, and a spirit of conciliation had been cultivated." On July 4, the entire

Convention gathered in the Reformed Calvinistic Church and listened to a sermon by Rev. William Rogers, who prayed for the "healing [of] all divisions and that "the United States of America may form one example of a free and virtuous government" (Federer, p. 250).

Recognize Moral Responsibility

Blame Shifting One of the ways to avoid responsibility is blame shifting. That is one of the oldest maneuvers in the human playbook. It is as old as Adam (Genesis 3:12). In America today, it is widely practiced and even contagious! An article in the *Harvard Business Review* reveals, "Blaming is contagious. A set of recent studies conducted in collaboration with Larissa Tiedens of the Stanford Graduate School of Business showed that merely being exposed to someone else making a blame attribution for a mistake was enough to cause people to turn around and blame others for completely unrelated failures... It appears that all you have to do to "catch" the blame virus is to be exposed to someone else passing the buck" (https://hbr.org/2010/05/how-to-stop-the-blame-game).

Blame shifting does not work. The *Harvard Business Review* article also says, "Research shows that people who blame others for their mistakes lose status, learn less, and perform worse relative to those who own up to their mistakes. Research also shows that the same applies to organizations. Groups and organizations with a rampant culture of blame have a serious disadvantage when it comes to creativity, learning, innovation, and productive risk-taking."

Other Maneuvers There are other ways of not assuming responsibility for one's choices, such as playing the victim or living a self-centered, self-serving, selfish life. In the fall of 67 AD, Paul wrote to Timothy, "In the last days, perilous times will come. For men will be lovers of themselves, lovers of money, boasters, proud, blasphemers, disobedient to parents, unthankful, unholy, unloving, unforgiving, slanderers, without self-control, brutal, despisers of good, traitors, headstrong, haughty, lovers of pleasure rather than lovers of God, having a form of godliness but denying its power" (1 Timothy 5:1-5).

In the U.S. today, we have freedom, but that freedom needs to be balanced with responsibility. In his book *Man's Search for Meaning*, Psychiatrist Viktor E. Frankl (1905-1997) wrote, "The Statue of Liberty on the East Coast should be supplanted by a Statue of Responsibility on the West Coast" (Frankl, p. 156).

Reestablish the Traditional Family as the Norm

Scripture God's design is that within a family unit, parents teach their children His Word (Deuteronomy 6:7-9). Beyond Bible-teaching churches, one of the greatest needs in America today is for fathers and mothers to teach their children to be morally responsible people. Righteousness exalts a nation (Proverbs 14:34). As was pointed out earlier, when America was first founded and immigrants, armed with a Judeo-Christian heritage, poured onto American soil, the social structure was such that living as a family was the norm. Obviously, that includes getting married rather than living together and having children out of wedlock.

A School of Psychotherapy Among psychotherapies, the Family Therapy school of thought, says that all things being equal, the major force in the development of any person is the family. The family of origin influences how a person looks, thinks, feels, and acts (Foley, pp. 465-466). Other theories of psychotherapy, such as the psychodynamic theory, agree, but it is the family therapy view that describes in detail what a functional family looks like.

The Family Therapy movement teaches that the qualities of a strong family include 1) Responding positively to challenges and crises rather than denying or distorting reality. 2) They have a clearly articulated worldview, often expressed in religious terms. 3) They communicate well, meaning they actively listen, affirm, and support, express their thoughts and feelings, and manage their differences. 4) They spend time together in planned and spontaneous varieties of tasks. 5) They make and honor promises to one another as well as take tasks and responsibilities seriously. As a result, there is a sense of belonging and respect for individual differences. 6) They know how to express their love and appreciation for one another (Jones and Butman, p. 353). If America had more families like that, many personal problems would be prevented.

One of the major problems in the decline of America is the decline in family living. Most children today grow up in a dysfunctional family. Dr. Broghammer says, "40 percent of American children are now born to unwed parents. Statistically, half of these couples will separate before their child is nine years old, placing the entire family at risk for anxiety, depression, or addiction. Even for traditionally structured families, modern life is challenging. American homes have fewer children but more square footage than ever before. Our quality time together has dropped precipitously: We spend time in separate rooms, doing separate tasks. According to Harvard sociologist Robert Putnam, we spent 43 percent less time at our family dinner table than we did 25 years ago. When we do sit down together, technology frequently interferes. Historically, the family has been the first society where children gain social identity and security. But our homes are becoming less stable, less intimate, and, consequently, less formative than ever before" (Broghammer, see bibliography).

Therefore, one of the greatest needs in America today is for parents to teach the Word of God to their children. May the Lord raise up such parents! That is not an impossible dream. He can do that.

Rethink Education

Public education needs to be more open to considering the fact that there is a God and that people are morally responsible. If the Senate can have a chaplain, who is paid by the government, to pray in the Senate, if the Supreme Court can open every session with prayer, if the Armed Forces can have a chaplain, who is paid by the government, to conduct religious services for military personnel, why can't public schools begin the day with prayer? If the Ten Commandments can be publicly displayed in the Supreme Court, why can they not be seen in public schools?

Admittedly, this issue is complicated today by the greater diversity of religions in the United States. If, however, it can be done in the Senate, the Supreme Court, and the military, why can it not be done in public schools? How about using a prayer similar to the one that opens the sessions of the Supreme Court, namely, "God save the United States and this Honorable Court?" Before it was ruled unconstitutional by the Supreme Court in 1962 (*Engel v. Vitale*), New York used the nonsectarian prayer, "Almighty God, we acknowledge our dependence upon Thee, and we beg Thy blessings upon us, our parents, teachers, and our country. Amen."

Regulate Some Economic Issues

Corporations As we have seen, the Bible supports certain concepts of capitalism, such as the private ownership of property, the accumulation of wealth, and making money by the use of money. In a capitalist system, some will own property, and some will not; some will accumulate enormous wealth, and some will not; some will use money to make money, and others will work for an hourly wage. The problem is that people who accumulate wealth have power that can be abused instead of properly used. From a biblical point of view, those with wealth and power have responsibilities. What is needed is responsible capitalism.

For example, Paul says, "Masters give your bondservants what is just and fair, knowing that you also have a Master in heaven" (Colossians 4:1). In the Roman world, slave owners had absolute rights over their slaves. Slaves were viewed as being only animated tools. The master could scourge and even kill his slaves. Slaves did not have the right to marry. If they did cohabit and there was a child, the child belonged to the master. Paul teaches that masters are to be just and fair. The motivation for this is that human masters have a divine Master in heaven. Masters have a Master who is no respecter of persons. So, they should not show respect for people. Because of the righteous character of God, treating people justly is morally right, even when it is not legally necessary. The master is still the master, but Christianity regulates all of their transactions with those placed under them.

In an article entitled, "Forget Socialism. The US Needs Responsible Capitalism," Bill George writes, "Responsible capitalism recognizes that companies have a clear purpose to serve society, their customers, and their employees as well as their investors...

Capitalists must take the lead in reforming capitalism from its unrestrained vices into its responsible virtues. When practiced responsibly, capitalism can be the greatest wealth creator and builder of societies and nations. But when wealth is hoarded by the powerful few at the expense of the many, people question the legitimacy of the economic system" (https://fortune.com/2019/05/06/socialism-ceo-leadership-responsible-capitalism/).

Paul told Timothy to "Command those who are rich in this present age not to be haughty, not to trust in uncertain riches but in the living God, who gives us richly all things to enjoy. Let them do good, that they may be rich in good works, ready to give, willing to share" (1 Timothy 6:17-18). All are to give, hourly wage earners (Ephesians 4:28) and the wealthy (1 Timothy 6:18), but the Scripture says more about giving of the wealthy than the wage earner.

Beyond enjoying one's wealth, Paul lists the duties pertaining to wealth. 1) The rich are to be rich in good works. It is possible to be materially wealthy and poor in good works. In the book of Revelation, the church in Smyrna was poor; nonetheless, they were rich before God (Revelation 2:9). On the other hand, the church at Laodicea was materially wealthy but spiritually bankrupt (Revelation 3:17; see also Luke 12:21). 2) Those who have money ought to be generous. (Philippians 4:14-16). They should be not only willing but ready to give. They should not need a great deal of persuasion. As Paul says elsewhere, "*So let* each one *give* as he purposes in his heart, not grudgingly or of necessity; for God loves a cheerful giver" (2 Corinthians 9:7). 3) The rich should think of their giving as sharing. The Greek word translated "willing to share" comes from the Greek word for "fellowship." Giving is a form of fellowship. It is not a superior giving to an inferior. It is one believer sharing with another.

Government As pointed out, the government's role in economics is to serve as an umpire to ensure the players play fairly. For example, the government should pass laws to prevent unfair business practices such as monopolies.

The other economic factor in the U.S. is that the federal government spends more than it collects in taxes. That is called *deficit spending*. Deficit spending has been going on for so long that On December 16, 2019, the *debt* of the U.S. was $23,053,720,112,278.14. That included what the government owes to investors (bondholders) and what it owes to itself (to pay its bills, the federal government has borrowed from the Social Security Trust Fund). That would be $75,878 for every man, woman, and child in the U.S. As of April 1, 2024, the debt of the U.S. was $30,278,646,895.828.99. That would be $91,047 for every man, woman, and child in the U.S. (For up-to-date figures, go to www.davemanuel.com/us-national-debt-clock.php.) As the US senator, Everett Dirksen, once remarked, "Pretty soon, you're talking about real money."

The Congressional Budget Office (CBO) projects that interest payments will continue growing rapidly, from $389 billion in the fiscal year 2019 to $914 billion in 2028. According to the World Bank, creditors do not worry about government debt until the debt is more than 77% of the GDP (Gross Domestic Product). In the first quarter of 2019, the U.S. debt-to-GDP ratio was 105%. (Tha is the $22.028 trillion U.S. debt as of March 31, 2019, divided by the $21.06 trillion nominal GDP.)

Thomas Jefferson said, "It is incumbent on every generation to pay its debts as it goes." For the current generation to borrow money that will have to be paid back by future generations is immoral. Imagine a neighbor putting a $75,000 debt on your credit card that you have to pay.

Moreover, nations collapse not only under decadence but also under debt. In 1826, John Adams said, "There are two ways to conquer and enslave a nation. One is by the sword. The other is by debt." Deficit spending and debt will eventually destroy the U.S.

There are four ways to decrease debt. The first is to cut spending. The Simpson-Bowles report recommended several ways to do that, but Congress ignored it. Sequestration tried to force the government to cut discretionary spending by 10%, but the debt continued to grow even with sequestration. The second is to raise taxes. According to the Laffer Curve, if Congress raises the tax rate above 50%, the additional revenue generated will be lower than before. The third is to drive economic growth at a faster rate than the debt, but Congress disagrees on how to grow the economy (increased spending versus lower taxes). The fourth is for Congress to shift spending to areas that create the most jobs, such as spending on public infrastructure (bridges and roads).

Neither the president nor Congress are willing to address this problem and the public is either unaware of it or ignores it. To bring public awareness to this problem, two things could be done. The first is to stop having income tax automatically taken out of people's paychecks and instead have everyone pay their taxes every month. The second is to have government spending at all levels (national, state, and local) posted on the internet and published in print once a month. Public awareness would result in political pressure to solve this problem.

Reinforce the Rule of Law

Politicians The rule of law has suffered at the hands of politicians and judges. Many politicians today do not lead society; they follow society. They make decisions based on polls, not principles. They focus on focus groups. Too many politicians are influenced by lobbyists. Then, there is corruption, including tax evasion and crony capitalism (government officials favoring one set of business owners over others).

Instead of politicians, the need is for statesmen officials who are committed to the concepts that made America great. America needs statesmen who will stand for what's right regardless of the cost or how long it takes us to get America on the right track. "At one point in British history, the abolition of slavery appeared to be a lost cause until a man of faith decided to fight because of his Christian principles. William Wilberforce fought for more than 40 years in a battle that turned even his friends against him. You could say he gave his life for the fight, dying just three days after learning that the Slavery Abolishment Act had become law" (Thomas, pp. 124-125).

Actual Judges Instead of activist judges making law, judges who interpret and apply the law need to be elected and appointed. Kupelian suggests that reclaiming America means " recalling or impeaching activist judges" (Kupelian, p. 242).

Reclaim the Sanctity of Life

The Scientific Perspective The biblical indications of the humanness of the fetus are confirmed by modern medical science. In the 1960s, the genetic code was unraveled. From the moment of conception to when the sperm permeates the egg, twenty-three pairs of chromosomes are complete. The sex, size, shape, color of the child's skin, hair, eyes, intelligence, and temperament are already determined. Between twelve and twenty-eight days after conception, the heart begins to beat. At four to six weeks, although the embryo is only a quarter of an inch long, the head and body are distinguishable and the brain waves can be measured. The skeleton, fingerprints, circulatory, and muscular systems are complete at eight weeks. At nine to ten weeks, the child can use his hands to grasp at his mouth to suck his thumb. By thirteen weeks, when the pregnancy is only one-third through, the embryo is completely organized, and a miniature baby lies in the mother's womb. He can alter his position, respond to pain, noise, and light, and have an attack of hiccups. From then on, he merely develops in size and strength.

Electrical brain waves have been recorded as early as forty days. Heartbeat is generally used to determine life. The heartbeat begins between the eighteenth and twenty-fifth day. If the fetus is not alive, why is he growing? If he is not human, what kind of being is he? If he is not a child, why is he sucking his thumb?

The Alternatives There are alternatives to abortion. As modern science has given us insight into the nature of the fetus, modern medical science has also provided a means of birth control. Other abortion alternatives, see "How to Deal with an Unplanned Pregnancy If Abortion Isn't for You" (https://www.healthline.com/health/alternatives-to-abortion).

Summary: Because the society of the U.S. has moved away from the things that made it great, what is needed for America to be great again is more biblically thinking Christians, Bible-teaching churches, functional families, public education open to God and personal morality, responsible capitalism, debt reduction, statesmen instead of politicians, actual judges instead of activist judges, and the use of alternatives instead of abortion.

Speak Up Jesus said, "For this cause, I have come into the world, that I should bear witness to the truth" (John 18:37). In the current environment, it is easy to be intimidated. Follow Christ. Speak the truth. Paul said, "For I am not ashamed of the gospel of Christ, for it is the power of God to salvation for everyone who believes, for the Jew first and also for the Greek" (Romans 1:16). "When innocent people are being led off to gas chambers, ovens, and other modes of execution—when unborn babies are destroyed in abortion mills—it is inexcusable to stand by and not seek to rescue them. It is also useless to plead ignorance" (MacDonald on Proverbs 24:11-12).

Just remember to speak the truth in love (Ephesians 4:15). The Lord invites us to "reason together" (Isaiah 1:18). Paul said, "A servant of the Lord must not quarrel but be gentle (2 Timothy 2:24) and "Let your speech always be with grace" (Col. 4:6). State your case clearly and give reasons for what you believe (1 Peter 3:15). Keep in mind, the objective is to win people to Christ and biblical truth. Speaking with anger and condemnation is not winsome. Agree to disagree, agreeably.

Tim Arndt suggests that on social media, Christians should stop making themselves look good, stop being rude, mean, and nasty, and stop attacking people. He adds, "When Christians are more well known for what they are against than what they are for, we lose" (see his complete article at https://relevantmagazine.com/culture/christians-lets-all-stop-doing-these-15-things-on-social-media/, accessed 11/9/2019).

Vote Believers in Jesus Christ should think biblically, live biblically, and vote biblically. This gets complicated because candidates are people, and people are not perfect. Finding a candidate with whom you agree on everything gets increasingly difficult, but some issues are clear, such as the sanctity of life.

Run for Office Kupelian suggests that the way to reclaim America is to "take over local government starting at the precinct level, run for Congress, encourage state legislatures to defy the Federal government when it usurps the states' constitutional Tenth Amendment powers, take our children out of government schools, or participate in peaceful civil disobedience" (Kupelian, p. 242).

Chapter 5

CONCLUSION: HOPE FOR THE U.S.

What has been presented is a brief sketch of the original Christian values that influenced society: people appreciated the Bible, acknowledged God, and accepted moral responsibility. As a result, the traditional family was the norm, the education system exposed students to Christianity, capitalism was the economic system, the rule of law was the law of the land, and the sanctity of life in terms of abortion was accepted.

Those issues influenced the society in America until the Bible was discredited, God was dethroned, moral responsibility was discounted, and, as a result, there has been a devaluation of marriage, a dumbing-down of education, a drifting away from capitalism, a decline in the rule of law, and the destruction of life in the form of abortion.

Is there any hope for the U.S.?

The Divided State of America

Welcome to the late, great U.S. This once great, united nation that respected the Bible, acknowledged God and believed in moral responsibility has now abandoned those fundamental, critical issues. The U.S. is no longer *united*. Instead of one nation under God consisting of a pluralistic society built on individual freedoms and equal opportunity, the U.S. is now *divided* between the so-called oppressors (the capitalists) and the oppressed (defined by race, gender, and sexual orientation).

In 2014, the Pew Research Center released its study of 10,000 adults, finding Americans more polarized than ever. Americans decide where to live, who to marry, and who their friends are based on what they believe. They are less likely to compromise. All of which means people in America are not listening to each other. No wonder there is such division.

Instead of the American dream of individuals exercising their free will to overcome obstacles to reach their dream, the dream is for the government to create social justice by the redistribution of wealth. As someone has said, "When half of the people get the idea that they do not have to work, because the other half is going to take care of them, and when the other half gets the idea that it does no good to work because somebody else is going to get what they work for, that is the beginning of the end of any nation!" (attributed to Adrian Rogers).

Hope for the Divided State

Is there any hope for America? Can America be great again? YES! An atheist can become a Christian. During World War II, Madalyn Mays Roths had an affair with William J. Murray Jr., a Catholic military officer in Italy. Both were married at the time. Murray refused to get a divorce. Madeline returned to the U.S., divorced her husband, and gave birth to a son (1946). She took the surname Murray and named her son, William J. Murray III (known as Bill), after his father.

Conclusion: Hope for The U.S.

In 1954, Bill's half-brother, Jon Garth Murray, was born. Their mother became an activist for atheism. In 1960, she filed a lawsuit challenging the constitutionality of compulsory Bible reading in public schools. She named her son William Murray III as the plaintiff. Madalyn's case, *Murray v. Curlett*, was folded into *Abington School District v. Schempp*. In 1963, the Supreme Court ruled that mandatory Bible reading and prayer in public schools was unconstitutional.

Later, Bill had a daughter with his high school girlfriend. In 1980, he became a Christian. His mother commented: "One could call this a postnatal abortion on the part of a mother, I guess; I repudiate him entirely and completely for now and all times. He is beyond human forgiveness." Bill became a Baptist minister. He became estranged from his mother, brother, and daughter, who were deeply involved in the American Atheists organization. Bill wrote his memoir, *My Life Without God* (1982), and several other books. He is now a conservative lobbyist.

In other words, the hope for the U.S. is that people like this atheist can trust Jesus Christ, who died for our sins and rose from the dead, for the gift of eternal life. That would be a great way to return to being a great nation.

Is there hope for America? Can America be great again? YES! Pro-choicers can become pro-lifers. As a college student, without knowing much about it, Abby Johnson got involved with Planned Parenthood, believing their goal was to help women at a difficult time in their life. She also had two abortions. She eventually became a Planned Parenthood director. She says, "I was very well versed in Planned Parenthood's talking points because I really believed them to be true. I was pretty convincing in that way. I became a very good salesperson for the organization, selling their highest revenue-generating product, and that was abortion." Then she was asked to assist in the abortion of a 13-week-old fetus. She says it was then, "I realized there weren't very many differences between me and this child in the womb. We both had the basic fight-or-flight human response. We were in different locations, and we were different sizes, but our humanity was the same. That's what caused me to ask: 'What are we doing here?' We might think we are helping women, but we are doing it at the expense of innocent human life. "As a result, she left Planned Parenthood and now serves as the CEO of the Pro-life Ministry, an organization that has helped more than 500 abortion workers leave the industry (https://www.americamagazine.org/politics-society/2019/01/14/abby-johnson-worked-planned-parenthood-now-she-leader-pro-life-movement).

Summary: Due to the departure from the original Christian-influenced society and the adoption of a secular view, the U.S. has become the divided states, but there is hope for America to be great again because the Lord can convert even the most radical individuals.

Theologian Wayne Grudem says, "There are two vastly different kinds of nations. The first one features increasing freedom, personal responsibility, and human flourishing. The second one features ever-increasing government control of every aspect of our lives, significant losses of freedom, and the implementation of many laws and regulations that are contrary to the moral teachings of Scripture (https://www.christianpost.com/voices/a-response-to-my-friend-john-piper-about-voting-for-trump.html).

Remember: "Righteousness exalts a nation" (Proverbs 14:34) and "Blessed is the nation whose God is the Lord" (Psalm 33:12).

Conclusion: Hope for The U.S.

As someone has said, "America's hope is not in an elephant or a donkey; it is in a Lamb." Before Jonah arrived, Nineveh was a secular, pagan city that was one sermon away from knowing the true and living God. Lord, give us a Jonah.

BIBLIOGRAPHY

Adams, Jay E. *Competent to Counsel: Introduction to Nouthetic Counseling.* Phillipsburg, N.J.: Presbyterian and Reformed Pub. Co., 1970.

Alinsky, Saul D. *Rules for Radicals.* https://archive.org/details/RulesForRadicals.

Allison, J. Robert. *The Age of Benjamin Franklin.* Course Guidebook. The Great Courses, 2018.

Atkinson, David M. *Leadership by the Book.* Dyer, IN: Grace and Glory Publishers, 2007.

Atwood, Craig D. *Handbook of Denominations in the United States*, 12th edition, edited by Frank S. Mead, Samuel S. Hill, Craig D. Atwood. Nashville: Abingdon Press, 2005.

Baldwin, Alice M. *The New England Pulpit and American Revolution.* Powder Springs, Georgia: American Vision Press, 2014 edition edited by Joel McDurmon.

Baldwin, Neil. *The American Revelation, Ten Ideals That Shaped Our Country from the Puritans for the Cold War.* New York: St. Martin's Press. 2005.

Barton, David. *Original Intent.* Aledo, TX: Wallbuilders, 2008.

Bloom, Allan. *The Closing of the American Mind.* New York: Simon & Schuster, 1987.

Breese, David. *Seven Men Who Ruled the World from the Grave.* Chicago: Moody Press, 1990.

Broghammer, Francie Hart. "Death by Loneliness," May 6, 2019. https://www.realclearpolicy.com/articles/2019/05/06/death_by_loneliness_111185.html (accessed 5/9/2019).

Bruce, Tammy. *The Death of Right and Wrong.* Roseville, CA: Publishing, 2003.

Cairns, Earle E. *Christianity Through the Centuries*. Grand Rapids: Zondervan Publishing House, 1981 reprint (first printed in 1954; revised in 1967).

Cooper, David L. *The Eschatology of the Visible Church*. Los Angeles: Biblical Research Society, 1945.

Davidson, Peter. "Achaemenid Empire," *Ancient History Encyclopedia*, February 11, 2011. www.ancient.eu/achaemenid_Empire/.)

Eidsmoe, John. *Christianity and the Constitution*, Baker Book House, Grand Rapids, MI, 1987; http://www.let.rug.nl/usa/biographies/william-blackstone/, accessed July 16, 2019.

Eerdmans' Handbook to the History of Christianity. Carmel, New York: Guideposts, 1977.

Frazer, Gregg L. *The Religious Beliefs of America's Founders: Reason, Revelation, and Revolution*. Lawrence, Kansas: University Press of Kansas, 2012.

Federer, William J., *America's God and Country Encyclopedia of Quotations*. Coppell, TX: FAME Publishing, 1994. This book is online at Google Books).

Foley, Vincent D. "Family Therapy," in *Current Psychotherapies*, edited by Corsini and Wedding, 4th ed. Itasca, IL: F. E. Peacock Publishers, Inc., 1989.

Foh, Susan T. *Women & The Word of God*. Grand Rapids: Baker Book House, 1980 reprint.

Frankl, Viktor, E. *Man's Search for Meaning*. New York: Washington Square Press, 1984.

González, Justo L. *The Story of Christianity*. Hendrickson: Peabody, Massachusetts, 1999.

Guelzo, Allen C. *The American Mind*. Course Guidebook. The Great Courses, 2005.

Holmes, David L. *The Faiths of the Founding Fathers*. Oxford University Press, 2006.

Horowitz, David. *Dark Agenda*. West Palm Beach: Humanix Books, 2018.

Irons, Peter. *The History of the Supreme Court*. Course Guidebook. The Great Courses, 2003.

Isbouts, Jean-Pierre. *Atlas of the Bible*. Washington, DC: National Geographic Partners, LLC, 2018.

Jones, Stanton L. and Richard E. Butman. *Modern Psychotherapies*. Downers Grove, IL: InterVarsity Press, 1991.

Kosmin, Barry A. and Seymour P. Lachman. *One Nation Under God: Religion in Contemporary American Society*, New York: Harmony Books, 1993, cited by Mark David Hall in "Did America have a Christian Founding?" posted at https://www.heritage.org/political-process/report/did-america-have-christian-founding#_ftnref3, accessed August 1, 2019.

Kroll, Wood. *Back to the Bible*. Sisters, Oregon: Multnomah Publishers, Inc., 2000.

Kupelian, David. *How Evil Works*. New York: Simon & Schuster, 2010.

Lindsell, Harold. *The Battle for the Bible*. Grand Rapids: Zondervan Publishing House, 1976.

MacIntyre, Alasdair. *After Virtue*. Notre Dame, Indiana: University of Notre Dame Press, 1984.

Millard, Catherine. *The Rewriting of America's History*. Chapel Hill, PA: Horizon House Publishers, 1991.

Muller, Jerry Z. *Thinking about Capitalism*. Course Guidebook. The Great Courses, 2008.

Olasky, Marvin. *The Tragedy of American Compassion*. Washington, D. C.: Regnery Publishing, Inc., 1992.

Petro, Bill. "In what ways did The Great Awakening influence the American Revolution?" www.quora.com/In-what-ways-did-The-Great-Awakening-influence-the-American-Revolution, accessed August 12, 2019.

Silk, Mark. "Mark Silk on the History of the Term 'Judeo-Christian.'" https://www.ncronline.org/news/opinion/distinctly-catholic/mark-silk-history-term-judeo-christian, accessed August 3, 2019).

Smith, Gary Scott. *Religion in the Oval Office*. Oxford: Oxford University Press, 2015.

Snyder, Michael. "40 Facts That Prove That America's Moral Collapse Is Spinning Wildly Out Of Control." April 5, 2019, accessed September 2, 2019. http://theeconomiccollapseblog.com/?s=40+Facts+That+Prove+That+America%27s+Moral+Collapse+Is+Spinning+Wildly+Out+Of+Control.

Solzhenitsyn, Aleksandr. "Godlessness: The First Step to the Gulag." Templeton Prize Lecture, May 10, 1983. http://orthochristian.com/47643.html

Stevens, Leon G. *One Nation Under God: A Factual History of America's Religious Heritage*. New York: Morgan James Publishing, 2014.

Thomas, Cal. *America's Expiration Date*. Grand Rapids, Michigan: Zondervan. 2020.

Twenge Jean M. *Psychology Today*, "The Real Reason Religion is Declining In America," https://www.psychologytoday.com/us/blog/our-changing-culture/201505/the-real-reason-religion-is-declining-in-america.

White, Lynn. "The Historical Roots of Our Ecologic Crisis." *Science* magazine, vol. 155, num. 3767, March 10, 1967. https://science.sciencemag.org/content/155/3767/1203/tab-pdf.

Witchel, Alex. "Father Rabbit." *New York Times,* November 22, 1992. https://www.nytimes.com/1992/11/22/style/father-rabbit.html.

Youmans, Elizabeth. "The Role of the Bible in Early American Education," June 22, 2017, http://darrowmillerandfriends.com/2017/06/22/bible-role-early-american-education/#_edn2

About The Author

G. Michael Cocoris is a gifted communicator. He can make even complicated subjects simple, clear, and practical. His breadth of experience has allowed him to relate to a wide range of audiences.

Michael received a Bachelor of Arts degree from Tennessee Temple University, a Master of Theology degree from Dallas Seminary, and a Doctorate of Divinity from Biola University. He traveled the United States for over a dozen years as a speaker. He has also been a seminary professor, visiting lecturer, and world traveler, including hosting tours to Israel and China.

Michael has pastored three churches, including a rural church when he was in seminary, an urban church, the historic Church of the Open Door, first in downtown Los Angeles and later in Glendora, California, and a suburban church, the Lindley Church in Tarzana California, a suburb of Los Angeles. While at the Church of Open Door, he had a daily radio broadcast.

Michael has written numerous magazine articles, mainly for *Biblical Research Monthly*. He has authored a number of books, including *Seventy Years on Hope Street, A History of the Church of the Open Door*; *The Spiritual Life, Clarifying the Confusion*; *Repentance, The Most Misunderstood Word in the Bible*; *Evangelism: A Biblical Approach*; *The Salvation Controversy*; *Lordship Salvation: Is It Biblical?*; *The Books of the Bible, the Subject, Structure, Situation, and Significant Verses of Each Book*; *Psalms, A Song for Every Situation, Each Summarized on One Page*; and *Psychotherapies: A Simple Explanation and Biblical Evaluation*. In addition, he was a contributor to *The NKJV Study Bible* and *Nelson's New Illustrated Bible Commentary*.

Michael is the pastor of the Lindley Church in Tarzana, California. He and his wife, Patricia, lived in Santa Monica, California.

www.ingramcontent.com/pod-product-compliance
Lightning Source LLC
Chambersburg PA
CBHW030521080526
44586CB00011B/287